SAINTS AND SINNERS

Prose & Poetry

Charles Péguy

Rendered into English by
ANNE AND JULIAN GREEN

CLUNY
Providence, Rhode Island

Cluny Media edition, 2019

Originally published in 1944 as *Men and Saints: Prose and Poetry*
by Pantheon Books, copyright © 1944 Pantheon Books

This edition is published under license of Preservation Books,
a non-profit corporation dedicated to promoting
the fair use, appreciation, and preservation of great works.

For more information regarding this title
or any other Cluny Media publication,
please write to info@clunymedia.com, or to
Cluny Media, P.O. Box 1664, Providence, RI 02901

VISIT US ONLINE AT WWW.CLUNYMEDIA.COM

ISBN: 978-1950970490

Cover design by Clarke & Clarke
Cover image: Gino Severini, *Le Boulevard*,
1911, oil on canvas
Courtesy of Wikimedia Commons

SAINTS AND SINNERS

Contents

POETRY

INTRODUCTION

IN THIS SECOND VOLUME of translations from Charles Péguy, I am, as in the first one, responsible for the poetry and, as before, have not attempted to give anything like a metrical rendering of Péguy's lines. It is not easy to state in a few sentences what Charles Péguy's poetry consists of or, indeed, why it is poetry. Its language is made up of everyday words, words which might sometimes appear almost worn out for having been used so often; yet those are the words which Péguy seems to prefer to all others, those he handles with greatest care, one might almost say: with piety, as if age and hard work had made them more venerable than the rarer words used by the educated. In Péguy's mind, a word is all the more beautiful if it is used by his charwoman, or by the bus conductor, or by the man who sweeps the streets of Paris with a large broom that makes a noise like a storm as it drives the dead leaves into the gutter. Péguy himself talks like those people, and he makes God the Father talk like them too. Neither is his thought lowered by such a process. What happens is that the simple language he uses is incredibly exalted and takes on a majesty which can only remind one of the Scriptures.

Such is the medium he uses: plain language so plain that in some unaccountable way it puts so-called literary styles to shame. With these everyday words, what kind of poetry does he write? To begin with, his poetry, on the printed page, looks like poetry, blank verse, modern in its irregularity. But if we read it aloud, it will seem to us that it is really prose cut up into lines of different lengths and that if these lines were to be put together again, we should have excellent prose. However, if we read it again and listen to the sound of it, and stop ever so little at the end of each line, we will catch a rhythm, not exactly the rhythm of speech, but what might be termed the rhythm of thought. And there, I believe, lies the essence of Péguy's poetry.

When his characters are allowed to speak, they make the most of their opportunity. Their conversation is an exchange of monologues. They go into a monologue as one goes into a trance and whatever remains outside of their monologue ceases to exist. Nor do they ever speak as if they expected an interruption or wished to argue their point. They are constantly making a profession of faith, and just as some people think aloud, they believe aloud. Their real audience is the sun and the moon and the stars, earth, man in general and finally the person with whom they may happen to be at the time. However there is nothing vague about these monologues; they are not the ravings of a dreamer; on the contrary, they come from as logical a brain as France ever produced.

Here we have another element in Péguy's poetry, an element which might be called the beauty of his reasoning. Péguy's reasoning goes from the particular to the general with a magnificent sweep which carries one along as only logic can do when it is enlivened by imagination. Its scope is apparently boundless. Like a true poet, Péguy instinctively, and logically, sees "a world in a grain of sand," but—and here your true "Normalien" comes out—he is ever ready to patiently trace all the steps from the grain of sand to its cosmic fulfillment, and he enjoys the trip immensely. No poet ever had a keener sense of the poetry of logic. This passionate love of reasoning, which he shares with his race, is probably one of the strongest intellectual links between France and ancient Greece, which France so often resembles, and we can well imagine the pleasure a platonic philosopher would have found in listening to God the Father's monologue on leprosy and mortal sin, surely as serious a monologue as was ever spoken, yet spoken with occasional smiles and sallies and, in one place at least, with an unmistakable wink.

Another characteristic of Péguy's logic is its beautiful emotional quality. It is strong but not unbending, and it has a way of suddenly moving us almost to tears. The heart has its reasons of which reason knows nothing, wrote Pascal, and in Péguy it is not only the head but the heart that reasons, a hard head and a big, generous, human heart. When the French peasant who is hewing wood in the forest stops to think of the time when he will no longer be among the living, he thoroughly examines the question and by slow degrees comes to the conclusion that his own existence is bound to the very existence of France, that he as an individual is merged into the greater individuality of his country, and that although he may cease to exist, France must and will go on. This he sees as a peasant can see it, a French peasant of the fifteenth century, as Joan of Arc's father might have seen it, but he sees it in such a way that, in 1944, we are more than ever struck by the inevitability of such a reasoning, we are listening to France herself telling us that she will not die, but live.

Turning to the contents of those mammoth poems which Péguy called *Mysteries*, it seems to me that of all the characters involved, God the Father is the most real if, for want of a better term, the word *character* can be applied to the first person of the Trinity. He is more real than Joan of Arc, because in a way he is more Joan of Arc than she could ever be herself, that is, all the qualities that are in her, he has to a super-eminent degree. We sometimes smile when we listen to him, but we are awed. He is never pompous, he never has to remember to be majestic, being majesty itself. He makes us feel like children and somehow he makes us feel a little better, a little more hopeful. He has a way of making clear what seemed irreparably involved in our spiritual life and with one word unties many knots. At the same time he lowers us somewhat in our self-esteem, he makes us a little ashamed, he makes us look a little foolish in our own eyes, but he does so in such a way that we are happier in consequence; he is eminently "le bon Dieu," the good Lord.

When God the Father enlarges on the subject of his universe, in the *Mystery of the Second Virtue* and in the *Mystery of the Holy Innocents*, he does so with poise and tremendous authority. He is certainly not lyrical. He blends the simplicity and wisdom of an old French peasant with the knowledge and shrewdness of a Church Father. There is something almost overwhelming about his simplicity, because it is the simplicity of truth and the simplicity of real wisdom. When he speaks of the stars, his stars, of the saints, his own saints, of Faith, of Charity, and of his "little Hope," he does so quietly, in fact so very quietly that our breath is taken away. It is not enough to say that he is great; he is great beyond any conception that we may have of greatness, he is the Lord, and because he is the Lord he can speak of creation not only with the authority of the creator, but at the same time with the humor and the matter-of-fact tone of the farmer who talks about his crops. He is immensely good and immensely forgiving; he grieves to punish the wicked; he is for justice with a strong leaning toward mercy; he loves all his children, particularly the French, for reasons which he explains at length.

Whatever this conception of God the Father may be worth theologically, it bears the stamp of genius and has its origin in the depths of a truly religious heart. The mere attempt to make God the Father deliver long speeches shows courage, and genius is a form of intellectual courage, the courage it takes to allow inspiration to carry one as far as possible, sometimes too far in the eyes of many. In literature as in other fields, the man who is afraid of going too far will never be among the great, and Péguy, with his firm, steady tread and that logical head of his, and his obstinate common sense, Péguy obviously went too far according to the world's method of reckoning distances, that is, he walked straight into the kingdom of Heaven.

The danger of such an undertaking, in the field of literature, is that it may turn out to be simply ridiculous, and to be ridiculous is dreadful. "Le ridicule tue" is a saying which every Frenchman hears repeated from his childhood on. If around 1905 a Frenchman had said to another Frenchman: "I am going to write a dramatic poem, the principal character of which will be God the Father," the comment would probably have been a smile. But it does not seem to have occurred to Péguy that he was running such a risk. This childlike man was of the same stock as the men who carved the portals of Chartres and Amiens, and he made God the Father speak just as he might have represented him above a doorway, six or seven centuries earlier.

"Faith is an oak rooted in the heart of France." If we wish to understand France, and to understand Péguy who spoke for France as few men have ever spoken, we must bear in mind that faith is an all-important element in the soul of that country. This gives us a clue to another aspect of Péguy's poetical world; I mean his vision of Calvary.

All ages have attempted to see Christ through the eyes of their great artists. Whether those artists followed the general trend of faith in their day, or whether they succeeded in imposing their own religious conception on the laity and clergy as well is a question which I cannot go into here, but the fact remains that they gave their world a visible reflection of what they saw with the inward eye. There is an early Italian Christ and there is a Flemish Christ of the fifteenth century, each of them intensely real; there is a French Christ contemporary of Joan of Arc and there is a German Christ of Dürer's time; there is also a Renaissance Christ and a seventeenth-century Christ; most moving of all, perhaps, there is Rembrandt's Christ. Each one is different, each corresponds to a particular form of piety and to a particular form of religious experience.

Péguy viewed religion with the eyes of a primitive, not an Italian primitive, to be sure, nor a Flemish primitive although he seems, at times, very close to Van der Weyden, but with the eyes of a French primitive of the fifteenth century, because he himself was a French primitive who had lost his way in the twentieth century. Now what characterizes French primitives is, above all, a deep and obvious sincerity of feeling and at the same time an equally deep tranquility of soul. They are contemplatives, but they never lose their heads in contemplation, they never let their nerves get the better of their reasoning powers, and they seldom suggest anything like ecstasy. If there be such a thing as an ecstasy of grief, we must look for it among the high-strung Sienese painters of the quattrocento or among sensitive and more obviously mystical artists such as the aforenamed Van der Weyden. The French are more placid. Their sorrow is sadness carried to an extreme, just as their inward happiness never causes their soul to lose its spiritual balance. When Péguy watches the Passion from the slopes of Mount Calvary, he sees it as a *donateur* might see it from the corner of a painting by the Master of Moulins or the Master of Avignon. He is moved, but he weeps in silence, neither does his weeping interfere with his prayers. Christ passes by, slowly bearing his heavy cross; Péguy neither faints nor tears his hair, he goes on telling his beads like a good Catholic, but his heart is breaking within his breast and when he tells us what he has seen, our own heart is very near breaking too, because he was so evidently there when those things took place.

This calm and stocky Normalien, this contemporary of Anatole France and Jaurès, knelt most assuredly on Calvary whilst the nails were being driven in our Lord's hands, and his faith, which was so admirably preserved from modern heresy, was the unsullied and undiluted faith of 1400. Probably the only flaw we could find in his vision of Calvary, if we were so minded, is the slight suggestion of an effort back of it all. Saint Thomas teaches that faith is partly a question of willpower. The will to believe is the beginning of faith; to a certain extent, it is faith itself, and Péguy's will was very strong. When he knelt and considered Christ on Calvary, he did not go into a trance, he rather willed himself into seeing. Indeed his vision of the Passion has a certain Ignatian quality about it. One is faintly reminded of the composition of place so strenuously advocated by that most willful of all saints, Saint Ignatius Loyola. But here the effort to see is blessed with a most moving glimpse of what must really have occurred.

The pictorial quality of Péguy's vision has never been properly stressed and one cannot help thinking that a study of the subject would bring forth much of interest to art and religion as well. To go back to the spiritual influence of artists on their times, it may live on for centuries and mold the thought of generations. We who are the heirs of many centuries cannot escape such an influence or, one might say, such an accumulation of influences. In a rather superficial way, it has made us richer. All of us who are interested in pictures and to varying degrees in the life of the soul have gone through phases which correspond in a general way to periods in the history of art. There were times, to be sure, when nothing but Botticelli could satisfy the demands we made on religious art. A little later, perhaps, we discovered Rembrandt, and Rembrandt made Botticelli seem finicky and even a little morbid; we eschewed everything that did not possess the gravity and the unmistakable air of inner truth which make the Dutch master so compelling. Then, for some reason, we drifted away from Rembrandt and turned to the Primitives. Only the Primitives had a really mystical view of Christianity, we thought; we were even somewhat intolerant on this point, we drew a line, say about 1360, beyond which no really religious hand ever wielded a brush, we were astonished and a little pained when people told us bluntly that they had never heard of our favorite painter, Barna.

And on we moved from phase to phase, learning a little, forgetting a great deal. There was, however, an influence which dominated all others, but this we did not care to admit because we were ashamed of it, in fact we loathed it, but loathing such an influence is like loathing the dampness, if you happen to be in equatorial Africa: no amount of loathing will cause it to go away; it is there, simply, and you breathe it in. In the same way, we breathed in Raphael. To this day, it is impossible to go into a church and not find some trace of that awful spell cast over religious sensibility by the great man whom our fathers called Sanzio. In an evil hour for Christianity, this magnificent genius stereotyped all the incidents of the life of Christ. He was the begetter of all the draped and nobly gesticulating figures we see in devotional books, of all the apostles and prophets with their faultless features and neatly brushed beards in illustrated bibles and on the walls of so many chapels. As Berenson so brilliantly pointed out, he changed a Hebrew world into a Greek one, and indeed when one comes to think of it, there is no essential difference between his scenes from the Old and New Testament and his School of Athens. But Raphael did much more, he infected and saturated the minds of millions with dull commonplaces about the Gospel. From one end of Europe to the other, he not only lowered the spiritual plane of art for generations, but made easy, and therefore suspicious, a certain approach to the realm of interior vision, he crowded the invisible with chromos. When a preacher enlarges on the Transfiguration, he unconsciously and irresistibly goes back to Raphael's vision of that scene, because Raphael is in his blood, although he may never have seen a Raphael in his life. Raphael is probably one of the most dangerous heretics since the Church began; his heresy is a subtle one which begins with a yawn and ends with nausea. His good intentions are as plentiful as they are demoralizing. He kills devotion with an almost infallible aim. Charity turns into a lump of ice under his nefarious gaze, and great though he was, the fact that he ever touched a paintbrush is the equivalent of one of those spiritual disasters from which the world has apparently not recovered.

I doubt that Péguy bothered much about painting or about Raphael's influence on the statuary sold in the pious shops of the rue Saint Sulpice, but whether he knew it or not, he was, as I have said, a French primitive, and because he was a primitive he fought with all his might against the dark angel of religious painting, he fought him simply by drawing in beautiful stiff lines and using colors which the Church itself seemed to have mixed for him.

It may be interesting at this point to indicate one of the sources of Péguy's inspiration. As we might have guessed, it was liturgical. Like his elder and greater brother, Francis Thompson, Péguy was a careful reader of the Catholic prayer book, that compact little volume which the French call their *paroissien* and which contains much of the spiritual wealth stored up by the Church since the early days of Christianity. He read the missal with the zeal of the convert. In a way he rediscovered it and studied its many pages with an eye which had become disaccustomed to its language. This allowed him to see things which habit kept Catholics of a longer standing from seeing for themselves.

One instance of what I mean is to be found in the ceremony of Holy Saturday, when the paschal candle is blessed and lighted. This ancient rite is known in English-speaking countries as the Blessing of the New Fire. It is as beautiful as it is old and the prayers read on that occasion are permeated with a feeling of happiness and even of exultation which lend them an almost lyrical quality. We expect them at times to break into a hymn, as if the very words called for music. This impression is heightened by a very moving use of repetitions. A few words from these prayers may he quoted here:

> This is the Paschal solemnity, in which the true Lamb is slain... This is the night in which Thou didst first cause our forefathers to pass through the Red Sea with dry feet. This therefore is the night which purged away the darkness of sinners by the light of the pillar. This is the night which restores to grace and unites in sanctity those that

> believe in Christ. This is the night in which Christ arose victorious from the grave… O wonderful condescension of Thy Mercy towards us! O inestimable affection of charity…! O truly needful sin of Adam, which was blotted out by the death of Christ! O happy fault, that merited so great a Redeemer! O truly blessed night, which alone deserved to know the time and hour in which, Christ rose again from the grave! This is the night of which it is written: And the night shall be enlightened as the day; and the night is my light in my enjoyments…

If, having listened to the beautiful music of those words, we turn to Péguy and read the last pages of his second *Mystery*, we can, I believe, catch an echo of the Catholic liturgy in his invocation of night, whom God the Father calls his daughter:

> You, night, are my great somber light.[1] I am glad to have created night… Night, my most beautiful invention… O night, O my daughter night, the most religious of my daughters, the most devout… Night, you are a beautiful invention of my wisdom. Night, O my daughter night, O my silent daughter at Rebecca's well, at the Samaritan woman's well, it is you who draw the deepest water from the deepest well. O night, you who rock all creation to sleep… O night, you who wash all wounds… At the Samaritan woman's well, you who draw from the deepest well the deepest prayer. O night, O my daughter night,

1. *Splendor nocturna*, says the Church.

> you who know how to hold your peace, O my daughter of the beautiful mantle...you who put the Child Jesus to bed every evening in the arms of the very Holy and Immaculate One. O my daughter sparkling and somber, I greet you...

There probably never was a Catholic more thoroughly enamored of the Church than Péguy, and yet he was remarkably free from any kind of bigotry. Bigotry is one of the besetting sins of converts; a bigot is a person who goes about in a sort of mental cage, but Péguy remained a free man until the moment he was killed; he never lost contact with humanity, he loved humanity, he considered himself, to a great extent, his brother's keeper (and as such assumed the right to shout at him and, if necessary, to kick him), nor did he ever lose his magnificent sense of humor. His greatest gift as a man and a poet was that of being able to speak intelligibly to all people, and to help them; his greatest gift was to give.

JULIAN GREEN

EDITOR'S NOTE

THE TITLE AND SUBTITLES are not Péguy's. Omissions in the text are indicated by dashes. The whole text is quoted from Charles Péguy's *Cahiers de la Quinzaine* (Paris, 1900–1914).

PROSE

THE HUMANITIES

Happy New Year

These New Year's greetings were written in 1905, a crucial year in the life of Péguy and of France. It was the year of the Morocco crisis and of Germany's intervention in the domestic affairs of France, when she requested, and obtained, the resignation of Delcassé, French Minister of Foreign Affairs. From this moment on Péguy had the premonition of the war in which he was to die. In the face of this future, he sums up his cultural heritage, and the civil and military obligations of a Frenchman forced to live under the system of armed "peace."

FOLLOWING THE CUSTOM of our fathers, let us exchange the season's greetings. Friends, let us exchange the season's greetings at the beginning of this year of good fortune or fatality. If we were ancients we might content ourselves with wishing that this year, new today, be a happy year. But as we are moderns, the inheritors of the four disciplines, Hebrew, Greek, Christian, and French, let us at least have the virtues of our vices. Let us remember that humanity has not only known Plato, that it has not only known this greatest philosopher of antiquity, but that it has also known the great modern philosophers: Descartes, Kant, Bergson.

Heirs as we are of ancient culture, not only to the extent to which we are able but even a little more than we deserve, let us wish this year to be a happy year and one that will be successful. But let us wish this without any pride, without any presumption, without any anticipation, without any arrogation. That is, let us believe that good fortune and happiness, considered as the successful issue of an event, are a capital element of all life, and let us not despise success, not that success which is called peace and the maintenance of peace, nor that success which is called victory. But let us wish it in such a fashion and in such terms that we do not call down upon our heads the jealousy of the gods, nor the vengeance of fate. Let us not be defiant, as those others are.

As much as we can, as much as we will and sometimes even a trifle more, we are the heirs of the Hebrew discipline, we are the heirs of the ancient Jews, we are, together with the modern Jews, the co-inheritors of the ancient Jews—at least together with certain among the modern Jews—we are friends with certain particularly qualified new Jews, those that are the most noble, the most devoted, the most worthy of their earthly eternity and of their incomparable race. We are the fellow-guests of the Jews, that is, eating today at the table of the same commonwealth. Let us receive this teaching from the Hebrew discipline, from the ancient and modern Jews: that the temporal salvation of humanity is of infinite price, that the survival of a race, that the earthly and temporal survival of a race, that the indefatigable and lineal survival of a race throughout all the waves of all the ages, that the maintenance of a race is a work, an operation of infinite worth, that the earthly and temporal immortality of a chosen race, even though this would mean simply a human race—that this maintenance and that this immortality is an object, a proposition of infinite worth which repays all sacrifices.—

We are, as much as we can and more than we deserve, the heirs of the ancient discipline. From the ancients let us receive this teaching: that we are citizens, that the state has its own value, an intrinsic value, an eminent value; that it is an institution, a plan of perfect worth, that the survival and that the conservation, that the immortality of the state reaching ever further, is a work, an operation which in itself is of perfect worth.

Heirs of the Christians, our fathers, let us receive this teaching of Pascal: that eternal salvation is of an infinitely infinite worth. That is to say, that while we will do all that is humanly possible to ensure the perpetuation, the survival of this people and the preservation of this state, we will scrupulously refrain from committing whatever is aggressive, remembering that all that pertains to holiness is of an infinitely superior order. The infinite distance between bodies and spirits measures the distance infinitely more infinite between spirits and charity. For charity is supernatural.

As Platonists we will know everything about our state, as Kantians we will know our whole duty. As Platonists, or as the heirs of the ancient Platonists, we will know everything about our Republic and we will know all of our laws. As

Kantians or as the heirs of the neo-Kantians we will know all of our moral obligations. But we will ask of the ancients that these moral obligations remain beautiful. We will ask of the Christians that these moral obligations remain holy, remain charitable. Of the Messianic we will ask that these moral obligations remain ardent. Of the Cartesians we will ask that these moral obligations remain distinct and clear. Of the Bergsonians we will ask that these moral obligations remain deep, interior and living, animated and true.

And reciprocally, we will borrow from the Kantians the proposition that the state be moral, that the Republic remain moral, that action, thought, race, holiness itself and charity, that life in its inwardness and profundity, that movement and reality remain humanly and absolutely moral.

As Frenchmen, heirs of our fathers, we will ask of the ancestor who waged the wars in Germany, we will ask of the many Frenchmen who waged war and who fought several times and who each of them died once for the liberty of the world, this form of courage which is so particular and so eminent that historians will be obliged to call it French courage; this courage essentially made of calm and clarity, this courage without bluff, this classical, essentially non-romantic courage.—

When a cultivated people is threatened with military invasion by a barbarous people, or by a barbarous government which has always led its people by the nose—when a free people is threatened with military invasion by a servile people—the cultivated people, the free people needs only to perfectly prepare its national military mobilization. And its mobilization once prepared, needs only to continue in the greatest peace and ease, while doing its best, its life of culture and liberty. Any change in this existence caused by the introduction of some element of fear, of apprehension, or even of expectation would already mean a successful attempt, a beginning of this military, barbarous, and enslaving invasion. Literally, it would mean a defeat, literally a conquest, a foothold for the invaders; because it would mean a beginning of barbarism and a beginning of servitude, the most dangerous of invasions: the invasion which crosses the threshold of inner life and which is infinitely more dangerous for a people than an invasion, than a territorial occupation.

In the same manner, when a simple citizen has prepared and holds in readiness his little individual mobilization, he needs only to continue to do his best as he leads the humdrum life of an honest man. For there is nothing in the world better than the life of an honest man. There is nothing better than the baked bread of daily duties.—

Above all, let us cling to this treasure of the humble, to this sort of implied joy which is the flower of life, this kind of healthy merriment which is virtue itself and more virtuous than virtue itself.—

It does not rest with us to provoke the event. But it rests with us to do our duty.

It is a dreadful anguish to foresee and to see collective death, whether it be that a whole people goes under in the blood of a massacre, whether it be that a whole people reels and succumbs in the retrenchments of battle, whether it be that a whole class dies at accelerated speed under the stress of the work which is supposed to give it food. And as humanity possesses no inexhaustible reserves it is a strange anguish to think upon the death of humanity.

The crises of teaching are not crises of teaching; they are crises of life.

Humanity Takes Leave

MAN MIGHT EASILY be reconciled to the idea of growing old, of passing and of disappearing, since doing so is his nature and doing so his destiny, had he but the consolation that though generations pass away humanity remains.

Unfortunately we no longer possess even this consolation; and we even possess the contrary certainty that humanity does not remain. Generations pass away and humanity passes away no less. Under our very eyes today Greek humanity is dying. What the invasions and the penetrations of no barbarians could achieve, what the persecutions of no Christian barbarians could achieve, what time even, that indefatigable demolisher, could not obtain, the short-lived triumph of a few political demagogies is accomplishing under our very eyes.—

During centuries great and powerful philosophies have battled for and against Greek culture, that is, for and against one of the essential cultures of humanity. An immense effort has been made to oppress, to bury, to annihilate ancient culture. A notable effort of preservation and continuance has been made by a certain number of Christians. An admirable effort of restoration has been made by the men of the Renaissance.—The great republicans—naturally, I do not speak of those of today—the republicans of the first, of the second, of the beginning of the third republic had seen very clearly how important it was for the preservation of the public spirit under a republican government that the humanities first of all be maintained.

Here is a very frequent phenomenon in the history of humanity. During centuries great philosophies fight for and against some great cause. And then, all is over. And, then, one day, while humanity has turned its back, a small band of scoundrels, grave-robbers, jackals and less than jackals come along. And the next day it is discovered that the said great cause has been strangled in the night.

This is what has just happened to us in the modern world with Greek. By a simple alteration, by a simple so-called reform of the secondary (or high school) educational programs—a whole culture, a whole world, one of the four cultures which have created the modern world—true, this last achievement is not their best—disappears, quite quietly and quite calmly right beneath our eyes from off the face of the world and from the life of humanity. Beneath our eyes, thanks to our solicitude, the memory of the most beautiful humanity vanishes. And in the second line, in the second degree, beneath our eyes, by our own doing, there perishes the whole effort of the humanists and of the men of the Renaissance. All that admirable sixteenth century will have fermented and made its restitutions in vain.—

Vainly we are told that Greek has taken refuge in college curricula, that it is fully preserved by a few university chairs, and in a few libraries. Of all the follies uttered in modern times, in which we have been lavish in uttering follies, this is the greatest. As well say that the ancient Egyptians live and come to life again in the sarcophagus-encased mummies of the basement rooms of the Louvre.—For a culture, for a history, for a life spent in the history of humanity, in short for a humanity, there lies an abyss between its figuring as part of a linear evolution in the memory and the teaching of a few professors and in a library catalogue, or, on the contrary, being incorporated by means of secondary studies, by humanities, in the whole body of artists, of philosophers, of poets, of writers, of savants, of men of action, of all cultured men, of critics even and historians, of all men of taste, of all sensible men, of all righteous and fruitful men, of all those men, in a word, who form a cultivated people within the people, within an ampler people. These two forms of existence are not of the same order. Existence in the body of those who produce for an entire people is a living existence. Existence on the shelves, on the shelves of a few libraries is an existence of death. Particularly in view of what modern libraries are like. A poet who lay in manuscript form, unknown, not understood, unread, unreadable in some lost monastery, was in himself neither a lost nor a dead poet. It was possible for some pious monk deserving of our eternal gratitude to care for him, preserve him, copy his works—in short, to hand him down to us. Therefore he was not dead. So he lived on for the future life of humanity. A poet, recognized, understood, classified, catalogued, who lies in print on the shelves of that barren library of the École Normale, and who would not have life elsewhere, who was not warmed in some heart, is a dead poet.

The Supplicants and the Supplicated

WITH THE MODERNS, a supplication is an act of abasement, a manifestation of platitude; prosternation becomes physical and moral prostration. To sum up in a word, the supplicant is an applicant. Such has been the infiltration of our political morals into the whole of life, into the whole of our social relations and such has been its coloration of it. Supplication in antiquity was an infinitely deeper thing, I might almost say, incomparably, infinitely truer, wholly different, wholly wise, wholly informed. In Homer, in the tragic authors, the supplicant is not an applicant; he is not a petitioner; he is not a man who abases himself, who humbles himself, even in a Christian sense. I need hardly say that he is not a modern who cringes. The ancient supplication, alone worthy of the word supplication and as such the only one worthy of holding our attention, the ancient supplication is in no sense, under no form, an act of platitude. Quite the contrary. On the contrary, read attentively one of those admirable ancient supplications, that supplication of the whole people at the feet of Oedipus, or what surely is even more admirable, what is perhaps the most admirable of all, the supplication of old Priam at the feet of Achilles. Read them over attentively: it is not the supplicated but, on the contrary, the supplicant who, at bottom, carries off the situation, the dialogue with a high hand. In all ancient supplication—the supplicated is a man who appears to have a fine position; he is even a man who, as we say, has a fine position, who has what is called a fine position. He is a king; he is a tyrant; he is a chief of a kind. In a war, he is a victor; he is a man of some preponderance, visible preponderance. Real preponderance? He is one of the mighty of the earth. In peace he is a rich man, a mighty man, a man who owns a lot of oxen. Let us describe him in a word: he is a happy man, a man who appears to be, who is happy.—He is a happy man. So, for the Greeks he is a man to be commiserated. The supplicated can speak only in the name of his happiness, at most in the name of happiness in general. This is little. This is nothing. This is less than nothing. This is even the contrary of all advantage. Happiness, understood in this sense as the success of an event, the rather insolent and almost abusive success, is for the Greeks the most infallible sign that a man is marked out for Fate—by Fate.—Innumerable Greeks, like the moderns, have desired, coveted, pursued with all their might the goods of this world, as much as have the innumerable moderns and by every kind of means: gold, power, the enjoyment of all pleasures. They were men such as we are. They preferred happiness to misfortune and, commonly, fine weather to rain. But nevertheless it remains, and it remains entirely true, that happiness understood technically as the success of an event is for the Greeks the most infallible sign that a man is marked by Fate. So that in this encounter, in this dialogue between the supplicant and the supplicated, which makes up the whole of an ancient supplication, it is the supplicant, no matter what he be, who he be, whether he be the beggar wandering along the highways, whether he be the wretched blind man, whether he be the outlaw, the exterminated, the citizen banished from the city, guilty or not guilty, the child expelled from his family, guilty or not guilty, this in the order of politics and in the order of peace, or, in the order of war, the prisoner, the vanquished, the feeble old man, whether it be the orphan or, on the contrary, the man who has been orphaned, the old man deprived of his descendants, it is always the supplicant who really has the advantage, who carries off the dialogue, who carries off the situation with a high hand.

As to the supplicated, he occupies a great, a high human position. But it is never more than a perfectly wretched human position.—And that is all. It is nothing. Particularly in comparison with other grandeurs.—What makes the weakness, the smallness of the supplicated is that he is only himself and his small portion of the human position. He does not represent.

The supplicant represents. He is no longer himself alone. He is not even himself any longer. He no longer exists. It is no longer he who matters. And that is why the other, the supplicated, must be on his guard. Despoiled of everything by the same event which precisely has made the dangerous happiness of the supplicated: a citizen without a city, an eyeless head, a fatherless child, a childless father, a stomach without bread, a pillowless neck, a roofless head, a man without possessions, the supplicant no longer exists as himself. And it is from that moment that he becomes formidable. He represents.

Because he has been handled, kneaded, manipulated by the human, superhuman fingers of the gods, suddenly he has become dear to the human, superhuman heart of the gods. Because he has been wax in the divine, superdivine fingers of fate he has become mysteriously dear to the divine, superdivine heart of fate. Because the hand of the powers above has weighed heavily upon him, by a singular reversal—not by a compensation—by a sort of filiation, rather, a superior childbirth, a particular adoption, the supplicant has become their protégé, their son. The gods and above them, behind them, fate, have taken away his father. But the gods have become his father. The gods and behind them, fate, the gods have taken away from him the city. But in a way the gods have conferred upon him their own city. The gods, subordinates of fate, have taken away his worldly goods. But those same gods have given him that good which no other good could replace, the gods have given him the first among all goods: he has become a representative of the gods.

There is no idea of compensation or even of justice: such an idea would be a Christian idea, at least a relatively recent idea, in a certain sense a modern idea.—There is a much deeper idea, a sentiment much deeper and far truer, as far as it is permissible to feel one's way a little among these mysterious, deep, true sentiments—a sentiment of life of art, of creation: that these men have proven themselves malleable men in the shaping hands of fate.—

Hence, without a doubt, comes the fact that the gods are so closely unified with man, that fate is so closely behind the man on whom she has once acted. When we read in the texts that *Zeus is hospitable*, that he is the *god of guests*, that guests come from Zeus, that a stranger comes from the gods, that the beggar, that the supplicant, that the poor wretch is an emissary of the gods, let us above all things refrain from believing that these merely are metaphors and embellishments. The moderns treat these grave questions with metaphors and embellishments. The ancients took these expressions literally. Quite truly. These wretched men, the supplicants, were like the ambulant witnesses of fate, doubly the works (let us not say doubly the creatures) of the gods.

That is why in ancient supplication the supplicant has the better part of the supplication. The other, the supplicated, is quite alone, quite naked and represents nothing. He, the supplicant, has behind him all of Olympus and what dominates Olympus itself. He represents a whole world of gods and even represents that which will bury the gods.

He represents destitution, woe, all misfortune, illness, death, the fate which will strike the gods themselves.

In all ancient supplication it is the supplicant that is master, it is the supplicant who dominates. Please note that what he asks can be refused him. If the other, the supplicated, wishes to aggravate his own case he is free to do so. But it is he, the supplicant, the man bowed at the feet of the supplicated who dominates the supplication, the act, the business of the supplication; he it is who is the master, who speaks a grand language, a masterly language and one which has come from afar, which has come from a quite other world.—

They are all of them ambassadors. And the ambassadors of a great king.—

In the face of such an elevation, what do the Greeks make of the meanwhile most important contrast between the just and the unjust, between innocence and crime? What becomes of the category of the just? What becomes of justice? What human honor or dishonor—or if this is too modern a term—what human advantage or disadvantage can compare with the advantage of having been chosen to become the plastic material of the gods and of her who dominates and who will model the gods themselves, and govern them in the slumber of death? And that is why the criminal supplicant, or to speak exactly, the former criminal—for since he is a supplicant he can no longer he a criminal—that is why the supplicant termed criminal is for the Greeks a man infinitely wiser, nearer the gods, more innocent than the wisest and the most innocent of happy men. To the happy man he can always give lessons, lessons in wisdom and innocence. The happy man is always guilty. At least guilty of being happy. But that is the greatest of crimes.

We do not run after the new; we do not run after the unknown; we do not run after the extraordinary; we look for the right and the fitting, and much that is right and much that is fitting was said before us, better than we ourselves would know how to say it.

We are as stupid as Saint Augustine and as Saint Paul, as Saint Louis and as Saint Francis and as Joan of Arc, and why not say it, as stupid as Pascal and as Corneille.—

We others, we make no progress. It is the moderns who make progress. We are stupid once and for all.

OLD FRANCE

It was in 1880. —Happy childhood. Happy innocence. Blessing on a good race. We thrived on everything. Everything succeeded with us. We received at all hands and it was always healthy food. We went to catechism, I think on Thursday, so as not to interfere with school hours. The catechism class was a long way off, in town, in our ancient parish of Saint-Aignan. Not everyone has such a parish. You had to walk up half the faubourg to the porte Bourgogne, go down half of the rue Bourgogne, turn left into that street which was called, I think, rue de l'Oriflamme and cross the cloister which was cold as a cellar under its heavy chestnut trees. Our young vicars told us exactly the opposite of what was told us by our young pupil-teachers.—We were not aware of it. The Republic and the Church dealt out to us diametrically opposite teachings. It mattered little as long as there were teachings. In instruction and in childhood there is something so sacred, in this first opening of childish eyes on the world, in this first glance there is something so religious that these two teachings were bound together in our hearts and we know very well that they will remain there eternally linked. We loved the Church and the Republic together and we loved them with the same heart, and this heart was the heart of a child, and for us the two were the wide world, and our two loves, glory and faith, and for us the whole was the new world. And at present… At present obviously we do not love them on the same level since we have learned that there are levels. The Church has our faith and all that belongs to her. But God alone knows how much we have remained bound by honor and heart to this Republic, and how much we are resolved to remain bound to it because it was one of the two purities of our childhood.

We were serious little boys of this serious town, innocent and at bottom already full of worries. We took seriously all that was said to us, both what our lay teachers said to us and what our Catholic teachers said to us. We took everything literally. We believed entirely, and equally, and with the same credence, everything contained in the grammar and everything contained in the catechism.—We have forgotten neither one nor the other. But this leads to a far less simple phenomenon. I refer to what took place within us regarding those two systems of metaphysics, since it is self-evident that a system of metaphysics must underlie everything.—

Everyone has a system of metaphysics. Patent, latent. I have said so often enough. Otherwise one does not exist.—The metaphysical system of our teachers was, in the first place, a system of educational metaphysics. But it also was, and above all, the metaphysics of science, the system, or at least a system of materialistic metaphysics (these beings so full of soul possessed a system of materialistic metaphysics, but after all that is the rule—and at the same time, it was idealistic, profoundly moralistic, and if one wishes, Kantian), it was a system of positivistic metaphysics, it was the famous metaphysical system of progress.—

We totally believed all that was told us. We were serious little fellows and assuredly sober. More than the rest, and to the highest degree, I had this disease. I have never been cured of it. To this very day I still believe all that is told me. And I strongly feel that I shall never change. To begin with, no one ever changes. I have always taken everything seriously. This has taken me far. So we believed totally in the teachings of our masters, and equally totally in the teachings of our priests. We absorbed completely the several or single systems of metaphysics of our teachers, and equally completely the system of metaphysics of our priests. I can say today without offending anyone that the system of metaphysics of our teachers has no longer for us or for anybody else any kind of a reality and that the system of metaphysics of our priests has taken possession of our being to a depth that the priests themselves would not have let themselves suspect. We no longer believe a word of what our teachers taught us, of the metaphysics which our teachers taught us. And we believe totally what is contained in the catechism, and it has become and it has remained flesh of our flesh.—

Our teachers were essentially and profoundly men of the old France. A man is not determined by what he does and still less by what he says. But in the deepest part of himself a being is determined solely by what he is. It is of little importance in this connection that our teachers in fact possessed a system of metaphysics which aimed to destroy the old France. Our teachers were born in this very house which they wished to demolish. They were the true sons of the house. They belonged to the people and that says all. We know very well that it is not their system of metaphysics which tore down the old house. A house never perishes but from within. It was the defenders of throne and altar that tore down the throne and, as much as they could, the altar.

Our old teachers were not only men of the France of yesterday. What they really taught us at bottom was the morality itself, and the essence, of the old France. I am about to astonish them greatly: they taught us the same thing as the priests. And the priests taught us the same thing as they did.—

Both of them and also our parents—all told us and taught us this stupid morality, which had made France and which today still prevents it from going to pieces. This stupid morality in which we have believed so much. To which, fools that we are and so little scientific, although facts have given us the lie, to which we cling desperately in the secret of our hearts. This fixed idea of our solitude, we inherit it from them all. All three taught us this morality, they told us that a man who works well and who behaves well is always certain to lack for nothing. The strangest of all is that they believed this. And the strangest of all is that it *was* true.

Our parents paternally and maternally; our teachers academically, intellectually, as laymen; our priests devoutly, piously; all of them with a great deal of heart taught, believed and *bore witness* to this stupid morality (our sole recourse, our secret strength): that a man who works as hard as he can and who has no great vice, who is neither a gambler nor a drunkard, is always sure of wanting nothing and, as my mother used to say, will always have bread in his old age. They all of them believed this with an ancient and deep-rooted belief, with an ineradicable, ineradicated conviction that a sensible and disciplined man, that a hard-working man was perfectly assured against dying of hunger. And even, that he was assured of the ability to provide for his family always. That he would always find work and that he would always earn his living.

All this old world was essentially the world of *earning one's living.*

To speak more exactly they believed that the man who confines himself to poverty and who has, even moderately, the virtues of poverty, finds in it a small, total security. Or, to speak more profoundly, they believed that daily bread was assured by purely temporal means, by the play itself of economical balance, to any man who, possessing the virtues of poverty, agrees (as in any case he ought) to confine himself to poverty. (Which in itself for them at the same time was not only the greatest happiness but even the only happiness that could be imagined: To be well housed in the little dwelling of poverty.)

One wonders where such a silly belief could have arisen, how it could have arisen.—Let us not look for a reason. This morality was not silly. It was true then. And it was even then the only true one. This belief was not absurd. It was founded on fact. And indeed it was even the sole one founded on fact. This opinion was not unreasonable, this judgment was not indefensible. On the contrary, it proceeded from the deepest reality of those times.

One often wonders where was born, and how was born, this old classical morality, this old traditional teaching of labor and security in wages, of security in reward, if only one remained within the limits of poverty, and its final consequence, security in happiness. But that is precisely what they perceived every day. As far as we are concerned, that is what we never perceive and we say: "Where on earth did they find all this?" And we believe (because they were schoolteachers and priests, that is, in a certain sense, schoolteachers still), we believe that this was an academic, intellectual invention. Not at all. No. On the contrary, it was reality itself. We have known times, we have been close to times, when this was reality. This morality, this idea of the world, this view of the world had, on the contrary, all the scientific sacraments. This morality was that of custom, of experience; it was practical, empirical, experimental, constantly accomplished in fact. This morality was "wise." This morality had seen the world. And here perhaps is the deepest difference, the abyss which lies between all this great ancient world, pagan, Christian, French, and our modern world, cut off, as I have said, at the date that I have said. And here once more we encounter this old proposition of ours that the modern world, by itself, and on its own side, by a single stroke, is in opposition to all the other worlds, to the men of all the old worlds blocked together, on the other side. We have known, we have been close to a world (as children we were part of it), where a man who confined himself to poverty was guaranteed in poverty at least. It was a kind of unspoken contract between man and fate; and fate never failed to fulfill its share of the contract, before the inauguration of modern times. It was understood that he who behaved whimsically, arbitrarily, that he who started gambling, that he who wished to escape from poverty, risked all. Since he started gambling, he might lose. But he who did not gamble could not lose. No one could suspect that times were coming, and that these times already were there, and that they precisely were modern times, when the man who did not gamble would lose all the time, even more surely than he who gambled.—

In their system, which was the very system of reality, he who acted defiantly, obviously risked all, but he who did not act defiantly risked absolutely nothing. He who attempted, he who wished to escape from poverty, he who gambled to escape from poverty, obviously risked falling into destitution of the most extreme sort. But he who did not gamble, he who confined himself to poverty, without gambling, without introducing the element of risk, also ran no risk of falling into destitution of any sort. The acceptance of poverty conferred a sort of diploma, constituted a sort of contract. The man who resolutely confined himself to poverty was never trapped within poverty. It was a retreat. It was an asylum. And it was sacred. Our teachers did not foresee, and how could they have suspected, how could they have imagined this purgatory, not to say this hell of the modern world, where he who does not gamble loses, and always loses, where he who is confined to poverty is unceasingly pursued in the retreat of poverty itself.—

It was understood that he who wished to come out of poverty risked falling into destitution. That was his business.

He broke the contract concluded with fate. But it had never been perceived that he who wished to confine himself to poverty was condemned to fall back perpetually into destitution. It had never been seen that fate would break the contract. They did not know, they could not foresee this monstrosity, this modern monstrosity, this trickery, this new trickery, this invention, this break in the rules of the game: that he who did not gamble continually lost.—

To us it was reserved, it was reserved for our lot that poverty itself should be unfaithful to us. To say all in a word, to us it was reserved, it was reserved for our lot to find that the marriage itself of poverty should be an adulterous marriage.—

They could not foresee, they could not imagine this monstrosity of the modern world (which already impended), they did not have to conceive this monster of a Paris which is the modern Paris, where the population is divided into two classes so completely separated that never before has so much money been squandered on pleasure and money refused to such an extent to labor.

And so much money squandered on luxury and money refusing itself to such an extent to poverty.

They could not foresee, they could not suspect this reign of money. They could all the less foresee it as their wisdom was ancient wisdom itself. The wisdom came from afar. It went back to remotest antiquity.—

There will always be rich and poor and *ye have the poor always with you* and the war between the rich and the poor takes up the greater half of Greek history and of many other histories, and money has never ceased to exert its power and it has not awaited the beginning of modern times to accomplish its crimes. But it is none the less true that the marriage of man with poverty had never hitherto been broken. And at the beginning of modern times it was not only broken, but man and poverty entered into an eternal unfaithfulness.

When one speaks of the ancients, with an eye to modern times, the ancient ancients and the ancient Christians must be understood together. It was the principle itself of ancient wisdom that the gods would unfailingly strike at the man who wished to rise above his station in life. But they struck far less generally at the man who did not attempt to rise above his station. It was reserved for us, it was reserved for modern times to see man smitten in his very station.

Seen with the eye of modern times, the ancient and the Christian fit together, belong together: the two antiquities, the Hebrew, the Greek. The Christian used to be an ancient. Until 1880. Today he has to be a modern. Such are the commandments of these temporal governments. Such are the powers of the world. It is undeniable that Christian ethics themselves have suffered this deep retortion. It was reserved for us to inaugurate this new state. In short, Christendom had little by little extended to the temporal order this saying that *he that humbleth himself shall be exalted* and that *whosoever exalteth himself shall be abased*. Thus understood, in this temporal sense, it is not only David's saying, *Deposuit potentes; et exaltavit*; it is almost the saying of antiquity itself. The saying of Hesiod and of Homer; and of Sophocles and of Aeschylus. It was reserved for us to inaugurate this regime where he who does not exalt himself is all the same abased.

To retrench, to banish from Christendom poverty, work, family, those three pillars of all life: what an attempt of organic decomposition, disorganization, dismemberment!

Christianity is undone if destitution, poverty, sickness are withdrawn from it. Reciprocally and together destitution, poverty and sickness are undone if Christendom, interior Christendom, Christianity are withdrawn from them. Christianity is the great regulator, the internal regulator of destitution, poverty, sickness. Destitution, poverty, sickness are surely a spring, a great internal regulator of Christianity.

Our socialism was a mystic socialism and a profound socialism, profoundly related to Christianity, a trunk grown from the old roots, literally then (or as ever), a religion of poverty.

THE MODERN WORLD

The World Is Against Us

We live in such barbarous times that when someone prints clean texts on clean paper with clean ink, everyone exclaims: He must indeed have time to lose! And money! We have no time, we have no more money, we have only our life to lose. We have been near to losing it; and we may be called upon to risk it again.

We live in such barbarous times that luxury is confused with cleanliness. When a workman tries to work properly he is accused of being luxurious. And as at the same time, and on the other hand, luxury and wealth always work sloppily, literally there no longer exists any medium through which culture either could be maintained or even through which it might seek to revive itself or merely defend itself. Through which it could return.

Those who have no money work sloppily under the name of sabotage; and those who have money work sloppily, a counter and different sloppiness, under the name of luxury. And thus culture no longer has any medium through which it might infiltrate. There no longer exists that marvelous unity true of all ancient societies, where he who produced and he who bought equally loved and knew culture.—

In ten years we have created a new firm,[1] almost universally known, very generally esteemed, very well rated, universally respected. We have created it and we have maintained it without ever having had a cent in reserve. Any man with some experience of economic realities will know, will be able to gauge the caliber of such an enterprise, and recognize it as a wager. But he will know too what such a wager costs, to be kept going for ten years, he will know that what is not taken out of money, what is not demanded of money, must always be derived somewhere: that for which there is no money, that which is not paid with money, must be paid for in the form of perpetual overwork, at the constant risk of life, in irreparable havoc to health.—

Let none deceive himself as to what lies ahead of us. Neither on the score of the near future of our *Cahiers* nor the near future of this country. In this state of barbarism, in this growing decay of culture, in this disorder of minds and morals, in this disaster of culture, the better our *Cahiers* are going to be, the less the access they will obtain to the general public, to what we might, in short, call the public.—

There is no cause for self-congratulation. We are defeated. The world is against us.—All that we have upheld, all that we have defended, morals and laws, seriousness and severity, principles and ideas, realities and comely language,

1. *Les Cahiers do la Quinzaine*—literally "*The Fortnightly Notebooks.*"

cleanliness, probity of speech, probity of thought, justice and harmony, accuracy, a certain dignity of demeanor, intelligence and good French, the revolution and our former socialism, truth, right, simple faith, good work, fine work, all that we have upheld, all that we have defended, falls back day by day before an increasing barbarism and decay of culture, before the invasion of political and social corruption.

No need to conceal this from ourselves: we are defeated. For ten years, for fifteen years, we have done nothing but lose ground. Today, in the decline, in the decay of political and private morals, literally we are beleaguered. We are in a place which is in a state of siege and more than blockaded and all the flat country is in the hands of the enemy.—

Today no one, no living man denies, no one contests, no one even dreams of concealing from himself that there is a disorder; a growing and extremely disquieting disorder; not indeed an apparent disorder, a state of fermentation which antecedes a coming order, but a real disorder of impotence and sterility; no one denies this disorder any longer, this confusion of minds and hearts, this coming distress, this menacing disaster. A debacle.

It is perhaps this condition of confusion and distress which, more imperiously than ever, makes it our duty not to surrender. One must never surrender. All the less since the position is so important and so isolated and so menaced and that precisely the country is in the hands of the enemy.

CHARLES PÉGUY

Probity

In the matter of the chase for worldly success, we have all picked our horses: The base souls have turned to baseness; the servile souls to servitude.

Idiots have turned to honesty. And what is more wonderful, they have a taste for it, the idiots, such a taste for honesty, for old-fashioned probity, that they cleave to it.

It is sometimes difficult for the "climber" to climb to the top because there is so much competition. But nothing is as easy as not to climb to the top if only one takes a little trouble. For in this case one crowds no one. Thus throughout the world one finds a certain number of young men, not very numerous—well, wily ones, particularly crafty lads, fellows who can't be taken in; old foxes who have chosen the career of non-success, the procession towards non-arrival. "They will enter the career when their elders are no longer there."[2] Nor will they have to wait that long. For their elders and they themselves will find plenty of room in this same career. According to rumor they are not at all cramped there, in fact they move at ease there, quite comfortably, without hate and without very much competition. At least, according to the reports of travelers, it seems to be a career in which elbows are not required.—

When a poor man has probity in his blood, he is lost. I mean lost for grandeurs. Of all the blemishes which attack the bones themselves and the marrow, this one is perhaps of all the most irremissible and that most stubborn. The man

2. Quotation from one of the last verses of the Marseillaise.

who does not succeed, who does not know how to go about it, who does not want to know how, fellows of our kind, in short, the idiot, the plain simpleton, *nidax vere simplex*, this good man knows very well, feels very keenly, since he came into the world, and even before it, because his father and mother were honest folk, that all his life he will get all the dirty jobs. Or at least, those admirable little jobs, which are taken hold of and which themselves take hold, pious and modest jobs, which the great of this world rate as dirty jobs. He knows full well that all his life he will be obliged to ruin his eyes correcting manuscripts and proofs.—

But this man likes it. He is so stupid that he does not even think of calling this probity, honesty, taste and passion for liberty. He execrates the very word of purity. Because of all sepulchers, whited sepulchers are those which remind him most of cemeteries. It is we, filthy pedants, who love to play at giving all this the names of virtues. With our mania for catalogues and indexes. That man needs neither our classifications, our encouragements, or our advice. All that he knows, this ignorant fellow, is that there are strings to be pulled which others pull all the time and that he will never pull, not even once, not even for a short quarter of an hour. Because this quarter of an hour would weigh on his stomach, would be impossible for him to digest.

All that he knows too, all that he finally knows, for he sees into the distance and far away, he sees to the end, is, that so his life will be, now and always, and that so will be his death.

CHARLES PÉGUY

To Know and To Believe

A PHILOSOPHER ON his deathbed recently said to the most faithful of his disciples, who made a note of his words for us. Having arrived at an advanced age this philosopher, a few moments before the moment of his death said approximately this: *"I know that I am going to die, but I do not believe it."* No doubt he meant by these words, as far as one can explain through analysis words so profound and so true, he meant no doubt by these words that he knew, that he foresaw, that he foreknew his approaching death with a full intellectual, historical, and scientific knowledge, implying an unquestionable historical and scientific certainty, but that he did not foreknow, that he did not foresee his own approaching death with an interior organic knowledge. One knows one's death, one does not believe it, or one does not believe in it. This, I think, is one of the most profound remarks that has ever been pronounced since death came into the world. And death has been in the world for a long while. This is a remark so profound, and one which reaches so profoundly to the most profound and the most essential sentimental springs, that it does not apply to death alone, that it is not true of death alone, but is true of all things, which are of the same degree of profundity as death, of the same order of greatness as life and death. It is not true of probity only, which is a virtue of race and of which the dishonest cannot have the least organic idea. It is true above all of destitution which is so closely related to death, being very exactly what the very rare expression of the Greek Antigone has indicated: a living death.

He who has not been tempted, in destitution, does not know what destitution and temptation are; and consequently he does not know what probity is, what it is to be honest. Or to speak quite exactly and to adhere strictly to the remark that we have reported, he can know it, but he does nothing but know it: he does not believe it and he does not believe in it.

GENIUS EXACTS THE patience to work—and the longer I live, citizen, the less I believe in the efficiency of sudden illuminations that are not accompanied or supported by serious work, the less I believe in the efficiency of conversions, extraordinary, sudden, and marvelous, in the efficiency of sudden passions—and the more I believe in the efficiency of modest, slow, molecular, definitive work.

The longer I live—the less I believe in the efficiency of an extraordinary sudden social revolution, improvised, marvelous, with or without guns and impersonal dictatorship—and the more I believe in the efficiency of modest, slow, molecular, definitive social work.

The Republic

I AM APPALLED when I see how estranged our young men have become from all that was republican thought and its mysticism. This is made plain above all by the fact that the thoughts which for us were thoughts have become ideas for them, that what was organic for us has become logic for them.—When a regime which was organic becomes logical, and after being alive has become historical, it is a regime that has caved in.

Today, the Republic is a matter of proof, of demonstration. While it was alive one did not have to prove it.

One lived it. When a regime can be demonstrated easily, commodiously, victoriously, one knows that it is hollow, that it has caved in.

"What does it matter," professional politicians tell us. "What does it matter to us," answer the politicians, "what can it matter to us. We have very good prefects. So what can it matter to us. It all works admirably. We are no longer republicans, true, but we know how to govern. We even know how to govern better, far better than we did when we were republicans. We have unlearnt the Republic but we have learnt how to govern. See the elections. They are admirable. They are always admirable. They will improve. They will become all the better, since it is we who make them. And since we are beginning to know how to make them."—The government makes the elections, the elections make the government. It is give and take. The government makes the electors. The electors make the government. The government makes the deputies. The deputies make the government. All oblige. The populations look on. The country is requested to pay. The government makes the Chamber. The Chamber makes the government. This is not a vicious circle, as you might believe. It is not in the least vicious. It is a circle, just that, a closed circuit, a closed circle. All circles are closed. Otherwise they would not be circles. This is not quite what our founders had foreseen. But our founders did not manage so magnificently at that. And then after all one cannot go on founding forever. It would be tiring. The proof that the Republic lasts, the proof that it endures is that it has already lasted forty years. It can go on for forty centuries. The first forty years are the most difficult ones. It is the first forty years that are hard. After that, one becomes inured. A country, a regime does not need you, it does not need mystics, a mystical doctrine, a mystical doctrine of its own. Such would be rather encumbering. For so great a journey, a good policy is required, that is to say a decidedly governmental policy.

They are mistaken. These politicians are mistaken. From the heights of the Republic forty centuries (of future) do not look down on them.[3] If the Republic has functioned for the last forty years, it is because everything has functioned during the last forty years. If the Republic is well-established in France, it is not because the Republic is well-established in France, it is because everything is well-established everywhere. There is in modern history—there are for modern peoples great waves of crisis, generally originating in France (1789–1815, 1830, 1848), which cause everything to quake from one end of the world to the other. And there are stages, more or less long, periods of dead calm, lulls which pacify all things for more or less long stretches of time. There are *epochs* and there are *periods*. We are in a period. If the Republic is solidly seated, it is not because it is the Republic,

3. Quotation from one of Napoleon's proclamations to his army during the Egyptian campaign: "Soldiers, from the heights of the Pyramids, forty centuries look down on you."

it is not because of its own virtue, it is because it exists, it is because we exist in a period of safe seatings. The duration of the Republic no more proves the durability of the Republic than the duration of neighboring monarchies proves the durability of Monarchy. This duration does not signify that they are durable, but that they have begun, that they are in a period, in a durable period. They are contemporaneous, they are steeped in the same kind of time, in the same bath of duration. They bathe in the same period. They are coeval. That is all that this proves.

In the Republic that lasts, it is not the Republic that lasts. It is duration. It is not the regime that lasts in it. But it is time that lasts in it. It is the tranquility of a certain period of humanity.—

They believe in regimes and that a regime makes or does not make peace and war, strength and virtue, health and illness, the safe establishment, the duration, the tranquility of a people. The strength of a race. It is as though one believed that the châteaux of the Loire cause or do not cause earthquakes.

We believe, on the contrary, that there are forces and realities infinitely more profound, and that it is the peoples, on the contrary, that make the strength and the weakness of regimes, and far less the regimes who make those of the peoples.—

We believe, on the contrary, that it is the peoples that make the regimes, peace and war, strength and weakness, the illness and the health of regimes.

The sole value, the sole strength of royalism, the sole strength of a traditional monarchy is that the king is more or less loved. The sole strength of the Republic is that the Republic is more or less loved. The sole value, the sole strength, the sole dignity of everything is to be loved. That so many men should have lived so much and suffered so much for the Republic, that they should have believed in it so much, that so many should have died for it, that they should have endured so many trials, often extreme, that is what interests me, that is what is real. That is what founds, that is what creates the legitimacy of a regime.

WE ARE ALWAYS being told of the republican degradation. When one sees what clerical policy has made of the Christian mystical doctrine, how can one be surprised by what radical policy has made of republican mystical doctrine. When one sees what the clerics have generally made of saints, how can one be surprised by what our parliamentaries have made of heroes. When one sees what reactionaries have made of holiness, how can one be surprised by what revolutionaries have made of heroism.

FOUNDERS COME FIRST. Profiteers come after.

We Are Defeated

WE ARE DEFEATED. We are defeated to such an extent, so completely, that I doubt whether history will ever have to record an instance of defeat such as the one we furnish. I do not know whether history will have ever known men as defeated as we are, beaten as we are, not shamed indeed, but shamefully beaten. Not by a defeat which brings glory, to which supreme honors go—but by the most stunted, ill-grown defeat that can be imagined; the most uncouth and ill-favored, the most vulgar which one has ever been able to achieve and which has ever been achieved and successfully achieved. To be defeated, that is nothing. It would be nothing. On the contrary it can be a great thing. It can be all: the final consummation. To be defeated is nothing: [but] we have been beaten. We have even been given a drubbing. In a few years, society, this modern society, before we have even had the time to sketch the critique of it, has fallen into a state of decomposition, into such a dissolution, such that I am assured that history had never seen anything comparable. I do not believe that selfishness in particular and the preoccupations of self-interest have ever fallen to a like degree of baseness. That great historical decomposition, that great dissolution, that great precedent which in a literary manner we call the decay of the Roman decadence, the dissolution of the Roman Empire and which it suffices to call, with Sorel, the ruin of the ancient world, was nothing by comparison with the dissolution of present society, by comparison with the dissolution and degradation of this society, of the present modern society. Doubtless, at that time there were far more crimes and still more vice(s). But there were also infinitely more resources. This putrefaction was full of seeds. People at that time did not have this sort of promise of sterility, which we have today, if one may say so, if these two words can be used together.

We are defeated. I believe, I am assured, that history has never recorded, has never had to record such defeated men as we, men defeated as much as we are. In less than a hundred and twenty years, the work not of the French Revolution, but the result of the abortion of the French Revolution and the work of the French Revolution is literally annihilated under the blows, under the weight, under the thrusts forward of the reaction, of universal barbarism. Completely. And not only nothing remains of it. No traces of anything. But no traces of promises even, nor of any fruitfulness to come.

ALL IS NOT lost, far from it, in the case of revolutionary atheism. Mistaken charities, flames of charity can burn deflected there, which some day will be led back to the right place. But there is nothing to be done with a reactionary atheism, with a bourgeois atheism. There is nothing to be expected, nothing must be hoped from, a reactionary atheism, from a bourgeois atheism. It is atheism without a spark, which will never be kindled, which will never blaze. It is atheism without charity and without even an imitation or counterfeit of charity. It is therefore hopeless atheism. Hope can move freely only with a certain minimal amount of charity. Hope, the gleam of hope, can be lighted only with a certain fire. From reactionary atheism, from bourgeois atheism, one can expect nothing but ashes and dust, because there all is death and ashes.

The modern world debases. Other worlds had other occupations. Other worlds had other ulterior motives and other ulterior intentions. Other worlds had other temporal pastimes, between meals. The modern world debases. Other worlds idealized or materialized, built or demolished, meted out justice or exercised force, other worlds created cities, communities, men or gods… The modern world debases. This is its specialty. I would almost say that this is its calling if the beautiful word *calling* were not above all to be respected. When the modern world debases, let us admit that then it is at its own work.

The modern world debases. It debases the state; it debases man. It debases love; it debases woman. It debases the race; it debases the child. It debases the nation; it debases the family. It even debases (always our limitations), it has succeeded in debasing what is perhaps most difficult in the world to debase, because this is something which has in itself, as in its texture, a particular kind of dignity, like a singular incapacity for degradation: it debases death.

THE DREYFUS CASE

The Dreyfus case, originally fought by the left against the right as a battle for justice against tyranny and prejudice, led to the victory of the socialist party, carried to political power on the crest of popular sentiment stirred up by the case. Péguy had been one of the most, ardent, and active "Dreyfusists," When, however, the socialist party, under the leadership of Emile Combes, used its triumph for the establishment of its own system of intolerance and injustice, inaugurated police supervision, denunciation (the famous fiches*), and a violent battle against the Catholic Church, Péguy was deeply disillusioned. Jaureè, leader of the French socialist party and his former friend, he now bitterly reproached with having succumbed to Combes' political demagogy.*

I SHALL ATTEMPT an exposition of what this immortal Dreyfus case in reality was. It was, like every self-respecting affair, essentially a mystical affair. It lived by its mystical doctrine. It died of its politics. That is the law, that is the rule. *That is the level of lives.* Every party lives by its mystical doctrine and dies of its politics.—

Our Dreyfusism was a religion. I use the word in its most literally exact meaning. It was a religious urge, a religious crisis—and I should even strongly advise anyone who would wish to study, to understand a religious movement in modern times—to take hold of this unique example. I add that for us, in our hearts, in us this religious movement was of Christian essence, of Christian origin, that it grew from the Christian root, that it flowed from the ancient spring.—The Justice and the Truth that we have so much loved, to which we have given everything, our youth, everything, to which we have given ourselves utterly during the whole time of our youth were not lifeless justices and truths, they were not the justices and truths of books and of libraries, they were not conceptual, intellectual justices and truths—but they were organic, they were Christian, they were not at all modern, they were eternal and not temporal merely.—And of all the sentiments which together urged us, in a state of trepidation, in this unique crisis, today we can own that of all the passions which urged us into this ardor and into this effervescence, into this dilatation and into this tumult, one virtue was at the heart of them, and that was the virtue of charity.—

We were heroes. It must be stated very simply for I do believe that no one will say it for us. Very exactly this is why and in what respect we were heroes. Everywhere in the world around us, everywhere we moved, everywhere we acted, where we still grew and where we were completing our formation, the question during the two or three years of that ascending curve was not at all to know whether *in reality* Dreyfus was innocent (or guilty). It was to know whether one would have the courage to recognize him, to declare him innocent. To proclaim him innocent. It was to know whether one would have the twofold courage. Firstly the first courage, the exterior courage, the already difficult gross courage, the social courage, the public courage to proclaim him innocent to the world, before the eyes of the public, publicly to testify in his favor. To wager on him, to risk on him everything that one had, the whole of painfully, poorly earned money, all the money of the poor and the wretched, all the money of small people, of misery and of poverty. One's whole time, one's whole life, one's whole career; one's whole health, one's whole body, one's whole soul; the ruin of the body, all the ruins, heartbreak, the dislocation of families, the disavowal of intimates, the turning-away of eyes, the mute or furious reprobation, mute and furious, isolation, quarantines of every kind. The breaking of friendships of twenty years standing, that is, for us, of immemorial friendships. The whole of social life. The whole life of the heart, in short, everything. Secondly the more difficult second courage, the inner courage, the secret courage of owning to oneself within oneself that he was innocent. To renounce for the sake of this man the peace of the heart.

Not only the peace of the city, the peace of the hearth. The peace of the family, the peace of wedlock. But the peace of heart.

The first of treasures, the only treasure.

The courage to enter for the sake of this man into the kingdom of incurable unrest.

And of a bitterness which never will be cured.

Our opponents will never know, our enemies could not know all that we have sacrificed for the sake of this man, and with what a heart we have sacrificed it. For him we have sacrificed our entire life, since this case has marked us for life. Our enemies will never know, we who have upset, turned this country upside down, our enemies will never know how few we were and under what circumstances we fought, under what thankless, precarious circumstances, under what circumstances of misery and precariousness.—We were, once more we were that handful of Frenchmen, who, under a withering fire, effect a breach in the line, lead an attack, capture a position.—

NOT ONLY WERE we heroes but, at bottom, the Dreyfus case can only be explained by that need of heroism which periodically seizes this people, this race, by a need of heroism which seized us then, us, an entire generation. These great movements, these great trials of an entire people are of one stuff with those other great trials: wars. Or rather, there exists for peoples only one kind of great temporal trial, which is war, and these great trials in themselves are wars. In all these great trials, in all these great emergencies, it is far more the inner strength, the violence of eruption which make the substance of history than it is the substance which creates and imposes the trial. When a great war breaks out, a great revolution, that other kind of war, the reason is that a great people, a great race has an impulse to break out; that it is fed up; namely that it has had enough of peace. It always means that a great mass feels a violent need, a great, profound need, a mysterious need for a great movement.—A mysterious need of making history. A mysterious need of a kind of historical fertility. A mysterious need to inscribe a great story in eternal history. All other explanation is vain, reasonable, rational, unfruitful, unreal. In the same way our Dreyfus case can be explained only by a need, the same, by a need for heroism which takes hold of a whole generation, ours, by a need for war, for *military* war and for military glory, by a need of sacrifice and even martyrdom, perhaps (no doubt), by a need of sanctity.—If we were, once more, an army of lions led by asses, then it is that we remained very precisely in the purest French tradition.

In reality the true position of the people who opposed us was, for a long time, not to say and to believe Dreyfus guilty, but to believe and to say that innocent or guilty, the life and salvation of a people, the enormous salvation of a people could not be troubled, could not be upset, could not be *compromised*, could not be risked for one man, for a single man. Tacitly they meant: the *temporal* salvation. And precisely our Christian mysticism culminated so perfectly, so exactly with our French mysticism, with our patriotic mysticism in our Dreyfusist mysticism that what must clearly be recognized is that our point of view focused nothing less than the eternal salvation of France. What indeed was it that we said? Everything was against us, wisdom and law, I mean human wisdom, human law. What we did was in the order of folly or in the order of holiness, which are alike in so many ways, which have so many secret correspondences, in the eyes of human wisdom, underneath the human scrutiny. We moved, we went at odds with wisdom, with law; at odds with human wisdom, with human law.—The others said: "A people, a whole people is an enormous combination of interests, of the most legitimate rights. The most sacred. Thousands, millions of lives depend on it, in the present, in the past, in the future; thousands, millions, hundreds of millions of lives constitute it, in the present, in the past, in the future, and by the action of history, by the deposit of history it safeguards incalculable interests. Legitimate, sacred, incalculable rights. A whole people of men, a whole people of families; a whole people of rights, a whole people of interests, legitimate ones; a whole people of lives; a whole race; a whole people of memories; all history, all the ascent, all the urge forward, all the past, all the future, all the promise of a people and of a race; all that is inestimable, incalculable, of infinite price, because it can be achieved once only, because it can be obtained once only, because it can never be achieved again; because it is a unique achievement; a people and particularly, namely, this people that is of a unique worth; this old people. A people has not the right, and the first duty, the strict duty of a people is not to expose all that, not to expose itself for one man, no matter who he may be, no matter how legitimate his interests or his rights. No matter how sacred, even. A people has never this right. One does not lose a city, a city is not lost for the sake of a [single] citizen. It was the very language not only of true civism and of wisdom, it was wisdom itself, antique wisdom. It was the language of reason. From this point of view it was evident that Dreyfus should sacrifice himself for France; not only for the peace of France but for the salvation itself of France, which he imperiled. And if he did not wish to sacrifice himself, of his own free will, if the need arose, he should be sacrificed. And we, what did we say? We said that a single injustice, a single crime, a single illegality, particularly if it is officially recorded, confirmed, a single wrong to humanity, a single wrong to justice and to right, particularly if it is universally, legally, nationally, commodiously accepted, that a single crime shatters and is sufficient to shatter the whole social pact, the whole social contract, that a single legal crime, a single dishonorable act will bring about the loss of one's honor, the dishonor of a whole people. It is a touch of gangrene that corrupts the entire body. What we defend is not our honor alone. It is not only the honor of our whole people, in the present, it is the historical honor of our people, all the historical honor of our whole race, the honor of our ancestors, the honor of our children. And the more we have of a past, the more we have of a memory (the more thus, as you say, we have of a responsibility) the more thus also we are obliged to defend it. The more we have of a past behind us, the more (precisely) we must defend it thus, keep it pure. *I will give back my blood pure as I received it.* That is the rule and the honor and the Christian urge. A single spot defiles a whole family. It also defiles a whole people. A single spot equally blemishes the honor of a whole family. A single spot equally blemishes the honor of a whole people. A people cannot remain passive before a wrong endured, imposed, before a crime so solemnly, so definitively countersigned. The honor of a people is a seamless coat.

What would this mean, unless one did not know a word of French, except that our opponents spoke the language of the interests of the State, which is not only the language of political and parliamentary reason, of the contemptible political and parliamentary interests, but far more exactly, far more loudly, is the language, the very respectable language of continuity, of the temporal continuation of the people and of the race, *of the temporal salvation of the people and of the race.* They meant no less. And we by a deep Christian reaction, by a very deep urge, simultaneously revolutionary and in the Christian tradition, following in this a Christian tradition in the deepest, the liveliest, the most orthodox sense, situated in the center and in the heart of Christianity, we meant no less than to rise, I do not say to the conception, but to the passion, to the anxiety for eternal salvation, the eternal salvation of this people; we aimed at nothing less than life in constant anxiety, in preoccupation, in mortal, eternal anguish, in a constant anxious care for the eternal salvation of our people, for the eternal salvation of our race. Quite at bottom we were the men of eternal salvation and our opponents were the men of temporal salvation. Such was the true, the real division in the Dreyfus case. Quite at bottom, we did not wish France to be constituted in a state of mortal sin. In this world, in this modern world, in any world, it is the Christian doctrine alone which to this extent, so deliberately, so totally, so absolutely insists upon holding temporal death as nothing, as an insignificant matter, as a zero in comparison with the cost of eternal death, and the risk of temporal death as nothing in comparison with the cost of sin, of mortal sin.

It is not easy to be a Jew. When they remain insensible to the appeals of their brothers, to the cries of the persecuted, to the wails, to the lamentations of their bruised brothers throughout the world, one says: "They are bad Jews." And if they merely open an ear to the lamentations which arise from the Danube and the Dnieper, one says: "They betray us. They are bad Frenchmen."

Thus you pursue them, you continually overwhelm them with contradictory reproaches. You say: "Their finances are Jewish, they are not French finances." And French finances, my friend, are they French?

The Jews are the victims of an optical delusion very frequent, very well-known in the other orders, in the order of optics itself. As one thinks about them always, at present, as one thinks of nothing besides them, as attention is always focused on them since the question of anti-semitism has been raised, as they are always in the public eye, they are very exactly the victims of this well-known optical delusion which causes us to see a square *white on black* as much larger than the same square *black on white*, that appears quite small. Any white square on black appears *much* larger than the same square *black on white*. Exactly thus any act, any operation, any square *Jew on Christian*, appears to us, seems to us much larger than the same square *Christian on Jew*.

To measure all the value, all the greatness, all the amplitude, the whole angle of this delusion, to correct this angle of error, to give back to us, to find once again justice and accuracy, there is a healthy exercise, excellent for intellectual and moral health, excellent for intellectual and mental hygiene.—It consists in applying the best of proofs, which is the proof by the contrary. It consists in retaining certain facts, numerous facts, as they happen all along, and to say, to ask of one self, to ask of their author: "What would one say if he were a Jew?" Not only does this exercise always give results but one is surprised to see how much result it gives, how it rectifies. Then one sees quickly, one reckons easily that the greatest scandals and the most numerous are not Jewish ones. Not by a long shot.

PORTRAITS

Bernard Lazare

Bernard Lazare, journalist, was one of the first to set in motion the press campaign for the revision of the sentence which had sent Dreyfus to Devil's Island in 1894.

THE PROPHET, IN this great crisis of Israel and all the world, was Bernard Lazare. Let us salute here one of the greatest names of modern times—one of the greatest among the prophets of Israel.—

I will paint the portrait of Bernard Lazare. Unquestionably he possessed elements of holiness, of sanctity. And when I use the word saint, let no one suspect me of speaking metaphorically. He had a gentleness, a kindness of heart, a mystical tenderness, an evenness of temper, an experience of bitterness and of ingratitude, a perfect digestion of bitterness and of in gratitude, a sort of goodness in the full face of reality, a sort of goodness perfectly awake and perfectly aware and incredibly deep. He had goodness in superabundance. He lived and died for the Jews as a martyr. He was a prophet. So it was natural that he should be buried prematurely in silence and oblivion. In a deliberate silence. In an organized oblivion.—

The Jews especially bore him a grudge, especially despised him because he was not wealthy. I even believe it was said that he was extravagant. That meant that they no longer had need of him. Perhaps indeed he did cost them a little; had cost them a little too much. He was open-handed.

Only, it might perhaps be taken into consideration that he himself was priceless.—

He had that truth toward himself which after all is paramount. Many persons can betray us. But it is a great deal, it is already a great deal not to betray oneself. Many policies can betray, can devour, can absorb many mystical doctrines. It is a great deal that mystical doctrines remain true to themselves.—

The honor of having given life to the Dreyfus case clung to his shoulders like an irremissible cope.—Everywhere precautions very decently were taken that perfectly quietly he die of hunger.—Nobody spoke about him. Those whom he had saved passed him over even more obstinately, more silently than all the others, thrust him into a more secret, more obstinate silence.—Those whom he had saved were the most prompt. He himself was perfectly aware of this. No matter how much one knows ingratitude to be the rule, each time it occurs it comes as a surprise. And it is always hard to swallow.

He himself was under no illusion respecting the men whom he had defended. Everywhere he saw policies, political men emerge, devour all, devour, dishonor his work.—

A small minority, a small group, an immense majority of poor Jews (there are a great many), of poor wretches (there are a great many), remained faithful to him, were attached to him with an attachment, a fanatical love, exasperated day by day by the approaches of death. Those loved him. We loved him. Already the rich no longer loved him.

Therefore I shall relate the story of his funeral.

I shall relate the story of his end.

I shall say how much he suffered.

I shall say how much he remained silent.

I STILL SEEM to see his short-sighted glance falling upon me, so intelligent and simultaneously so good, of such an invincible, such an intelligent, such an enlightened, such an enlightening, such a luminous gentleness, of such an untiring, such an informed, such an enlightened, such a disabused, such an incurable goodness. Because a man wears a pince-nez well settled on a thick nose, barring and setting glass before two kind, big, near-sighted eyes, modern man is not able to recognize, is not able to see the glance, the fire lighted fifty centuries ago. But I have been close to him. I alone have lived in his intimacy and in his confidence. One should have heard, one should have seen this man who naturally believed himself to be a modern! One should have seen that look, one should have heard that voice! Of course he was very sincerely an atheist. At that time it was not only the dominant metaphysical system, it was the encompassing metaphysical system, that which one drew in with each breath, a kind of climatic, atmospheric metaphysical system; which was self-understood, as good breeding is self-understood; and moreover it was understood, positively, scientifically, victoriously, that this system was not a *metaphysical* system; he was positivistic, scientific, intellectual, modern, in a word all that was proper; above all he would hear no talk about metaphysics. One of his favorite arguments, the one which he always served up to me, was that Israel—since among all the peoples it was the one which believed the least in God—obviously was the people most easy to rid of ancient superstitions; and therefore this would be the people that would show the way to the others. The excellence of the Jews came, according to him, from the fact that they were by anticipation the most freethinking of peoples. And underneath this and inside this, a heart that beat to all the echoes of the world, a man who pounced upon a newspaper and who, over four pages, over six, eight, over twelve pages, with a single lightning glance fastened on a line, and in this line there occurred the word *Jew.* A creature who blushed, turned pale, an old journalist, an old stager of journalism who blanched at a small news item that he found in this paper, at a fragment of an article, at a short article, at a cable, and in this news item, in this paper, in this fragment of an article, in this short article, in this cable there occurred the word *Jew.* A heart that bled in all the ghettos of the world, and perhaps more in the disrupted ghettos and scattered ghettos, like that of Paris, than in the closed ghettos, in the excluded ghettos. A heart that bled in Romania and in Turkey, in Russia and in Algeria, in America and in Hungary, in all places where the Jew is persecuted, which is to say, in a certain sense, everywhere. A heart that bled in the East and in the West, in Islam and in Christendom. A heart that bled in Judea itself, and a man who made fun of Zionists. Such is the Jew. A tremor of anger and that was for some wrong suffered in the valley of the Dnieper. Also what our Powers did not wish to see—that he was the prophet, the Jew, the leader—that, the least of Jewish peddlers knew, saw, the most wretched Romanian Jew. A tremor, a perpetual vibration. All that is needed for death at forty.

Not a muscle, not a nerve but was held taut for a secret mission, perpetually quivering for the mission. Never did a man consider himself to this extent the leader of his race and of his people, responsible for his race and for his people. A being perpetually taut. Not a feeling, not a thought, not the shadow of a passion that was not taut, that was not commanded by a commandment fifty centuries old, by a commandment delivered fifty centuries ago. An entire race, an entire world on his shoulders, a race, a world of fifty centuries on bowed shoulders, on rounded shoulders, on sagging shoulders. A heart devoured by fire, by the fire of his race, consumed by the fire of his race. Fire at heart, a flaming head, *and the burning coal on the prophetic lip.*—

It must be considered that this was a man—as I have very precisely said, a prophet, for whom all the mechanism of power, the interests of State, the temporal powers, the political powers, the authorities of all orders, political, intellectual, even rational did not weigh an ounce set against a revolt, against a movement of the conscience itself.—For him they did not exist. He did not even despise them. He ignored them, and even more. He did not see them, he did not take cognizance of them. He was near-sighted.—They were not of his rank, of his degree, of his degree of greatness, of his greatness.—Never have I seen a man believe, know to such an extent that the greatest temporal powers, that the greatest bodies of State stand, exist only by grace of interior spiritual powers.—Thus he had a secret affection, a friendship, a deep affinity with the *other* spiritual powers, even with the Catholics whom he deliberately fought. But he wished only to fight them with spiritual weapons, in spiritual battles. He did not wish that there should be done to others what others had done to you, but which one did not wish them to do to you. "The clericals have been pestering us for years," he said and more energetically still, "but pestering the Catholics at present is not to the point." Never has there been seen a Jew so little partisan, thinking so little about, contemplating so little the law of retaliation. He did not exactly wish to return good for evil, but most certainly justice for injustice.—

Fundamentally he did not like, he could not bear to have the temporal interfere with the spiritual.—That organs as coarse as the government, the Chamber, the State, the Senate, so foreign to all that is spiritual, should lay the fingers of their hand upon the spiritual, that for him was not only a gross profanation but even more, an exertion of bad taste, an abuse, the activation, the abuse of a most singular incompetence. On the contrary he felt in himself a secret, a singular complicity of spiritual competence, if needs be, with the Pope.—

I have never seen a man believe so deeply, have so deep a conviction, that a man's conscience was an absolute, an invincibility, an eternity, a freedom, that it was opposed, victoriously, eternally triumphant, to all the grandeurs of the earth.—

I SHALL RELATE his death and his long and cruel illness and all his slow and yet so rapid journey towards his death. That sort of ferocious illness. So relentless. As though it were fanatical. As though it itself were frantic. Just like himself. Just like ourselves. I know of nothing so poignant, so startling, I know of nothing so tragic as this man who, bracing himself with all that remained to him of strength, barred the road to his victorious party. Who in a desperate effort which broke his own body attempted, undertook to stem the tide of victory and its abuses, the abuses of victory.—I still see him in his bed. This atheist, this professional atheist, this official atheist in whom reverberated with a strength and an incredible gentleness, the eternal Word; with an eternal strength, with an eternal gentleness, which I have never found anywhere equaled. I still have upon me, in my eyes, the eternal goodness of his infinitely gentle gaze, this goodness which was not impulsive but poised, aware. Infinitely disabused; infinitely aware; infinitely insurmountable. I still see him in his bed, this atheist overflowing with the word of God. In death itself the whole weight of his people still weighed upon his shoulders. One could not tell him that he was no longer responsible for it. I have never seen a man thus burdened, so much burdened with a burden, with an eternal responsibility. Precisely as we are, as we feel ourselves responsible for our children, for our own children in our own families, quite so much, exactly so much, he felt himself responsible for his people. In the most atrocious suffering he had but one anxiety: that his Jews of Romania be not craftily overlooked in that movement of condemnation that a few European publicists then undertook against the excesses of Oriental persecutions.—

He had been told falsehoods about his illness, falsehoods upon falsehoods. How much did he believe? He, like everybody else, pretended to believe. How much he believed—that is the secret of the dead. *Morientium ac mortuorum.* In this incurable cowardice of the modern world where we dare tell a man everything save what interests him, where we do not dare tell a man the greatest piece of news, the news of the arrival of the only important payday, we have lied ourselves so often, we have lied so much to so many of the dying and to so many of the dead that it is to be hoped that when our turn comes we will not believe entirely in the lies which are told us. So he pretended to believe in them. But it was impossible to read in his beautiful, gentle eyes, in his great, big, clear eyes. They were too kind. They were too gentle. They were too beautiful. They were too clear... It was impossible to know whether by a miracle of (temporal) hope, he still hoped for himself, or if it was through a miracle of charity for us that he pretended to hope.—

I shall tell the story of his funeral. Who we were, how few there were in this procession, in this funeral procession, in this faithful grey cortege descending and passing through Paris. Right in the middle of the holiday season.—A few, the same frantic, the same fanatical Jews and Christians, a few rich Jews, very rare, a few rich Christians, very rare, poor and wretched Jews and Christians, themselves in rather small number. In short a small troop, a very small troop. Like a sort of decimated company that crossed Paris. Wretched foreign Jews, I mean foreign to the French nationality, for there was not a Jew from Romania who did not know him for a prophet, who did not hold him a true prophet. For all these poor wretches, for all these persecuted he was still a flash of lightning, a rekindling of the torch which eternally does not go out.

I FEEL NO need of unifying the world. The more I see of the world, the more I discover that free men and free events are varied.

Dreyfus

HE HAS NOT died for himself; but several died for him. Others died for him.—

He never ruined himself for his own sake. He would never have ruined himself for the sake of another. But many went to their ruin for his sake.—

It was the greatest of fatalities that precisely this man should have constituted this affair, that he should have been irrevocably thrust into a public event, and precisely the most public event. He had perhaps all the private virtues. Doubtless he would have made a very good businessman. Why did he have to go and become a captain? What business did he have in the offices of the General Staff? What business had he to have a reputation, to acquire a celebrity, a universal fame? Victim in spite of himself, hero in spite of himself, martyr in spite of himself. Celebrated in spite of himself, he betrayed his fame.—Mysterious destination of the people of Israel. So many others who desire fame are obliged to stay quiet. And he, who would have liked to stay quiet, was forced to the vocation, was forced to the attack, forced into fame. Here is a man who was a captain. He thought to be promoted to a colonel or perhaps a general. He was promoted to Dreyfus. How do you expect him to get his bearings? Yet he needs had to get his bearings, yet it was his duty to get his bearings. He was improvised a pilot, helmsman of an enormous ship that he did not know how to steer, that he did not know how to direct. Nevertheless he was responsible for it.—Suddenly appareled, appareled in spite of himself in an enormous dignity, in a martyr's dignity, he acquitted himself lamentably. And what is most fatal, most painful, most tragic is the fact that we cannot help having to call him to account for it.

He who is chosen must move forward. He who is called must answer. This is the law, this is the rule, this is the level of heroic lives, this is the level of lives of holiness.—Whoever has had the world in hand is responsible for the world. We *must* call him to account. To account for this immense battle that he has lost. Against his will he found himself engaged commander-in-chief, more than that, the banner of an immense army in an immense battle against an immense army. And he lost this immense battle.—He who loses a battle is responsible for losing it. We cannot but call him to account for the public morals, of France, of *Israel itself*, of the humanity to which he belonged for a moment.

Singular destiny. He was invested, constituted in spite of himself a public figure. So many others have wished to become public figures, and have paid the price, and have been inexorably thrust back by the reality of history. He was invested, constituted in spite of himself a man of fame. He had everything that he did not wish. But he that is invested must advance.

So many men, thousands and thousands of men, soldiers, poets, writers, artists, men of action, victims, heroes, martyrs, so many men, thousands and thousands of men have wished to enter into public action, have wished to become, to make themselves public figures. And they have paid the price. They have put into it genius, heroism, efforts without number, incredible efforts, terrific efforts; terrific sufferings; whole lives and such lives of genuine martyrdom. And nothing, never anything. And he, without doing anything, in spite of himself in a few weeks, he became the man of whom the whole of humanity has heard the most; his name has become the name, he has become the man whose name everybody has oftenest repeated, has oftenest celebrated since Napoleon died. What a hundred battles gave to the latter, he received in spite of himself. And he was none the prouder for it.—

This tragic situation reminds me of a remark made by Bernard Lazare. One must always go back, one always goes back to a remark made by Bernard Lazare. This remark will be the decisive pronouncement on the case. Because, coming from its greatest prophet, it has a bearing on the victim himself.

Dreyfus had just returned. Dreyfus had come back and almost instantly, with the first happenings, the first negotiations, the first contact, everyone suddenly had the impression that there was a flaw somewhere, that all was not quite right, that he was as he was but not as we had dreamed him to be. Already then a few grumbled. A few, secretly, then publicly, accused him. Secretly, publicly, Bernard Lazare defended him. Sharply, obstinately, tenaciously. With that admirable voluntary blindness of those who really love, with that invincible obstinate blind fury with which love defends a being who is wrong, obviously wrong, publicly wrong. "I don't know what they want," said he, laughing but not laughing, laughing outwardly but inwardly not laughing, "I don't know what they ask. I don't know what they want of him. Because he has been unjustly condemned, everything is asked of him, that he have all the virtues. He is innocent, that already means a great deal."

The disregard of Israel for prophets, and despite this the guidance of Israel by the prophets: this is the whole history of Israel.

The disregard of sinners for saints and despite this the salvation of sinners by saints, this is the whole of Christian history.

The disregard of Israel for the prophets is only to be equaled, is only to be compared, although most different, with the disregard of sinners for saints. One can even say that the disregard of Israel for the prophets is a *symbol* of the disregard of sinners for saints.

Jaurès

Jean Jaurès, French socialist leader, founder of L'Humanité, *the daily organ of the socialist party. Led the socialist party in its campaign for the rehabilitation of Dreyfus.*

THE LAST TIME that I saw Jaurès was during precisely those months when he was preparing the publication of *L'Humanité.*—I am betraying no secret in recounting that Jaurès came to see me, at great intervals, at the printing office, in those days. From Passy to Suresnes through the wood, the road is beautiful. Jaurès, who at that time worked a great deal, far too much, at his articles for the *Petite République*[4] and above all at his enormous Socialistic History of the French Revolution—Constituent Assembly, Legislative Assembly, National Convention—four enormous volumes at least, if I remember rightly, *in quarto*, color of ox-blood, could not always very well stand so much work. Who else could have stood it, in his place? He felt the need, because of excessive work, heaviness in the head and a congested condition—he is full-blooded—congested eyesight—all the ailments of those who read, who write, and who correct proofs, he felt the need of taking a regular walk in the afternoon, a rather substantial walk afoot. The Bois is one of the monumental beauties of Paris. And the rather firm roads are good under foot. It takes thirty-five minutes to walk from Passy to Suresnes without hurrying. At great intervals Jaurès used to come and fetch me at the printing office. I was

4. Daily newspaper.

almost always to be found there. Together we used to set forth along well-curved roads and along straight avenues, I sometimes having to return to the printing office to finish my day's work, while on other occasions seeing him home for me was a way of returning towards Paris.

Those persons who sometimes have reproached me for having treated Jaurès with excessive indulgence obviously did not know the Jaurès whom I knew during these vociferous walks. We could meet and talk and walk honestly together. Without any compromise of any kind. Without cession on the part of one of the other. He had been, under the best possible conditions, one of our collaborators. And finally, at that time, he was Jaurès. And I was under no obligations to him. In the capacity of a contributor he had provided us with very good copy. In the capacity of chief editor I had printed editions of his copy such as he has never had since, such as he will never have again. Besides I do not know through what obscure premonition of later developments, or through what obscure penetration of deep, actual realities, through a wise management of this oratorical intercourse, I had always scrupulously conducted myself so that I owed nothing to my illustrious partner. Not only had I never asked of him one of those friendly services, one of those good offices which commit an honest man. Eternally. But I had always managed our literary business relations, and all others, I had always governed even my own sentiments in such a manner that my credit account always overlapped my debit account by a rather wide margin. There are, in life, such deep presentiments.

Exactly as at that time presentiments overcame me, anticipating later sadness, so today and reciprocally—memories assail me, recalling universal illusions forever lost. Who at that time would not have been attached to him? And who, once attached, would not have remained so? His ancient and authentic fame of the incipient Dreyfus case, strengthening, doubling his more ancient and no less authentic socialistic fame, still bathed him in a splendor of kindness. It was the time when it was public knowledge that Jaurès was kind. Others could deny his possession of other qualities, but all argument invariably ended thus: "He is kind. Undeniably, he is kind." And this was also the period, those four years, when, not being a deputy, having left the parliamentary world, almost completely the political world, he really occupied in this country a position which he has never regained.

A rather great number of persons reproach me with having retained a secret tenderness for Jaurès which even transpires, which is to be detected above all in my most justifiable severities. That is because they never knew a Jaurès that I knew perfectly in those days, a Jaurès who was a good walker and a good talker, not the perspiring and red-faced Jaurès of smoky public meetings, nor the Jaurès, alas, red-faced and become clumsily elegant, of the drawing-rooms of the republican defence; but a Jaurès of the open air and of autumnal woods, a Jaurès such as he would have been, had he never experienced ill luck, and whose footsteps rang on the hard soil of the roads. A Jaurès of the clear and golden hazes of the commencements of autumn.

A Jaurès who, although he had come to us from the foothills of the Cevennes and from the banks of the Garonne, perfectly appreciated the perfect beauty of French landscapes. A Jaurès who admired and who knew how to look at and how to see those marvelous trees of the Ile-de-France turned golden by the autumns of those times. A Jaurès who, standing by the frail railings, made of cast-iron or some such metal, of the Suresnes bridge, looking towards Puteaux, admired, knew how to admire, all of the industrial beauty of this part of the Seine. Or, looking in the opposite direction, planted upright to face the river, looked at, admired, registered, saw as a Frenchman the curved and noble river flowing at the foot of the admirable lines of hills. He explained all this to me. He always explained everything. He knew admirably how to explain by discursive, eloquent, conclusive reasons. Demonstrative reasons. That is what ruined him. A man who is so gifted for the explanation of everything is ripe for all surrenders. A surrender is essentially an operation by which one settles down to explain instead of to act. And cowards are people crammed with explanations.

I have known a poetical Jaurès. A common and long-standing admiration, derived in part from our university studies, united us in the same veneration of the classics and of the great poets. He knew some Latin. He knew some Greek. He knew an enormous amount by heart. I have had this good fortune and this has not been given to everyone—I have had this good fortune to walk by the side of Jaurès while he recited, declaimed. How many men have known the poets through the resounding voice of Jaurès? Racine and Corneille, Hugo and Vigny, Lamartine and even Villon, he knew all that everyone knows. And he knew a lot of what everyone does not know. All of *Phèdre*, it seems to me, all of *Polyeucte*. And *Athalie*. And *Le Cid*. He would have made an admirable Mounet,[5] if adverse fortune had not insisted in making a politician of him. He had been attracted to classic style perhaps chiefly by a Toulousan taste for Roman eloquence. And I must have been attracted to it a little more perhaps by a French taste for Greek purity. But in those times one did not infuse bitterness into these slight differences. Minds were united. One was not so critical. Although he was originally from Toulouse, he rose easily, perfectly, naturally to the intelligence and the taste of those perfect poets of the Loire valley and its environs, that are the marrow of French genius: du Bellay, the immortal Ronsard. He knew the sonnets. When you are old, at evening, candle-lit.[6] God grant that these compromising revelations harm him little in his constituency.

Mishaps occurred only when, remembering that as a *normalien*[7] he had begun by being a brilliant Ph.D., he undertook to play the philosopher. Then these conversations became disastrous. One day I had the misfortune to tell him that we very regularly attended M. Bergson's course of lectures at the College de France, at least the Friday course. I was sufficiently imprudent to give him to understand that this course must be followed if one wished to be in the know. Immediately, in less than thirteen minutes, he delivered himself of a discourse on Bergson's philosophy, of which he did not know and of which he would not have understood the very first word. It was all there. But he had graduated in

5. Mounet was a well-known tragedian of the Comédie Française.

6. The first line of one of Ronsard's "Sonnets to Helen."

7. Normalien, a boy who has studied at the École Normale.

the same class with M. Bergson from the former École Normale, the one called superior. That sufficed him. This was one of the moments in which he began to alarm me.

He was so eloquent that often he stopped, in spite of himself, mechanically, in order to be still more eloquent; and whether he walked or whether he stopped, people in the street often stopped to watch him talk. Not everybody did know him although he was the most famous man in France, and then in all the radiance of his glory. But whether one knew him or whether one did not—and since we are on the subject of confessions—in my foolish vanity as a young man, as a young socialist, as a young Dreyfusist, I was secretly flattered to be publicly the public, the public-man of a man so famous and so great an orator.

So THE LAST time, the last time that I saw Jaurès under these conditions, and I have never again seen him under any other conditions, was precisely during the months when he was preparing that newspaper which has become *L'Humanité*. There are old people who still remember all that was expected of this newspaper while it was in preparation. Jaurès's newspaper! Then the years to come would be filled. For years, everyone had very well known, everyone indeed had said that Jaurès would end by founding his own newspaper. At last one would have, at last one would see Jaurès's newspaper. One waited. One held one's breath. It would be a newspaper such as never had been seen. In short, Jaurès's newspaper! This term meant everything. One would see what Jaurès' newspaper would be like! There were rumors concerning the title.

It was at that time when, reaching the printing office a short while after lunch, the printers said to me: "Do you know, Jaurès came here to look for you." Those printers were not a little proud to give me this message for the reason that the veneration which former subjects had for the king of France was nothing in comparison with the sentiments entertained by our modern citizens for the great leaders of their democracy.

At that period it had been a very long time since I had seen Jaurès, that is, since he had been reelected deputy.[8] His surrender to the Combist demagogy and shortly after, his complicity in the Combist demagogy, had put the finishing touch to a separation of which the starting point could he traced to the very beginning of our relations. However when the printers gave me the message that Jaurès had called to ask for me, I said to myself that, after all, I was the younger, quite a young man in comparison with him, that in consequence I owed him respect and that I should give him precedence, that our former relations had never been anything but decent and highly honorable, that their memory would always be precious to me, that I could therefore, that I should make the next step myself. I put in an appearance at his house, if I remember correctly, next morning. There is not a single house at which I have visited once, where it is impossible for me honorably to return. Few public men can say as much.

I went to his house. At the time I thought that he had something to communicate to me. He had not. He was an entirely different man. Grown older, changed, one cannot

8. At the elections of 1902.

say how much. This final meeting was sinister. It is a great pity when two men who have shared a certain kind of life, after a long and definitive interruption of their intercourse meet again or are brought back by circumstances into the external conditions of this old life. No juncture as much as this sort of *rapprochement* leaves on the heart the dusty and hollow imprint of the vanity of miscarried destinies. He went out. I nevertheless accompanied him. We walked. He took letters to the post office, or telegrams. We walked and walked through the cold avenues of the sixteenth *arrondissement.* When we reached the statue of Lafayette, or thereabouts, he stopped a cab to do an errand. At the moment of leave-taking I felt keenly that it was for the last time. A movement of feeling, almost of remorse, made me feel that I could not thus leave him. At the moment I shook his hand for the last time, returning to what had been in my mind since the day before and since the beginning of my visit, I said to him: "I thought that you had come to see me yesterday at the printing office to talk to me about your newspaper." A little hastily he said: "No." A few moments before he had said to me in an exhausted tone of voice: "I run about, try to see people." He was weary and appeared so: "You can't get people going. They are played out. People aren't worth much." He was tired, bowed, wasted. I have never seen anything of anyone so sad, so distressing, so distressed as this professional optimist.

Did he at that moment have, and had he for some time already had, as the result of these efforts, a premonition of the atrocious life into which he was about to step. This day, this period were of prime importance in his life. Forever he quit the free life, the honest life, the open air life of the simple citizen; forever and irrevocably he was to plunge, to take the plunge into politics. He was overwhelmed with a great sadness. He was the spectator of his own decay. And as he was naturally eloquent, in his heart he complained most eloquently.—I said to him: "Listen. You know well that I am not asking you to let me collaborate on your newspaper. My whole life belongs to the *Cahiers*. But I have around me, or in short, there are a certain number of young men working for the *Cahiers* to whom you could give work. They are not famous. They do not chase after glory. But they are earnest. And they possess the virtue which has become the rarest of all in modern times: loyalty. Those who surround you are not conspicuous for their loyalty. And as for me, you know through what crises, through what straits the *Cahiers* have passed during the last five years: Not one of my collaborators has let me down. That in itself is more important than anything I have published. Doubtless this is the first time that this event has occurred since the foundation of the Third Republic." He was embarrassed. I insisted.—Whereupon he began to raise his arms to Heaven slightly, with an air of distress: "You know very well how it is. I had a full staff before beginning. It is easier to have contributors than to find financial backers."

That I already knew. A final handshake. Heavy, crumbling, he got into that loitering cab. I have never seen him since.

THERE IS NOTHING so mysterious as those secret preparations which await man at the threshold of all life. All is decided before we are twelve years old.

When I was small I believed that groups worked. Today we know that groups do not work. They create agitation.

Paris

Temporal capital of the world, intellectual capital—and spiritual capital still, always, in spite of everything, spiritual capital. *The city which has suffered most for the temporal salvation of mankind.*

Odious city of the greatest chirruping, and respectable city, respectful city, when one wishes, city of the most total silence, of the most infinite, of the most eternal, of the most authentic silence.

Of the greatest of goods: silence.—

The city of gambling, of gossiping, and of entertainment. City of the greatest elevation, of the greatest contemplation, of the greatest meditation. City of the greatest prayer.

City where they manufacture, city where they foment and where they bake, as bread is baked, city where germinates and rises the most of this substance of elevation, in that form of elevation, of contemplation, of meditation. Of prayer.

City where they sell the greatest amount of vice, where the greatest amount of prayer is given away.

Where you have that friendly Luxembourg garden practically to yourself. And yet there are a great number of you who have it thus entirely to yourselves. And in

September the sun has such a delicate, such an ambered savor; a savor akin to the peace of a *reposoir*.[9] And the sunlight is of such a rare quality after the subtle, after the transparent haze of a September morning, and so tranquil. Of a clarity so pure and so motionless, of an admirable soft warmth like that of leave-taking, calm, having the odor of a fruit, the scent of an autumn rose—and not yet that of the great dry leaf; the passage from outdoors to indoors, from open air and broad sunlight to the intimacies of the hearth, the approach of winter evenings—poignant, double-faced sentiment, expectation and fear, hope, calm, with perhaps a dash of regret.—

City of perdition. City of salvation.—

For us French, the city of France the most French, the most profoundly, the most essentially, the most authentically, the most traditionally French.—

And for everybody, the city that is the most insupportably cosmopolitan in the world; an orgy of nations; the most common crossway in the world; the caravansary of peoples; the most ancient of modern Babels; the confusion of tongues; the most modern of ancient Babels; a boulevard where everything is spoken excepting French. Particularly when people set themselves to talking Parisian.

The most international city in the world and the only really internationalistic one, the thoroughfare and sojourn of the peoples of the earth, of all the peoples; and a national city, even narrowly so, and nationalistic.

---

9. A *reposoir* is an open-air altar erected in Catholic countries during the procession of Corpus Christi, on which to rest the Holy Sacrament.

City of the most order and of the most disorder; of the greatest order, the only one which is truly real; apparently of the greatest disorder, really of the greatest disorder, the only fruitful one.

City of unrest, of incurable unrest and of vicissitudes, of perpetual tribulations, of essential tribulations, of the essential tribulation.

The most pagan of cities. The most Christian. Certainly the most Catholic.

City apparently the most readily seduced, where all the follies, where all the jokes, where all the nonsense, where all the insanities, where all the foolishness, where all the stupidity in the world, where all the prides, where all the futilities, where all the vanities of the earth immediately and automatically find a haven. More than a haven, a temple. A gracious reception, a trustfulness, an incomparable splendor. Unique. City of infatuation, of the silliest, of the most indefatigable. But the man who benefits by this infatuation would be a fool to trust in it. For immediately after, it is a city which automatically rids itself of the mud, of the rash, of the scum of all infatuation.

The most motionless of cities. And the one that is least slavish. Which is never led.—

For madmen the maddest of cities, the city of most madness; for the wise the wisest of cities, the only city of the most, of the greatest wisdom. The only wise city. Of the only wisdom. The greatest antique wisdom in the world since the ruin of the ancient world, since the death of Athens (and Rome). And the one with the greatest amount of Christian faith. The most faithful Christian faith.

Capital of lust. Capital of prayer. Capital of faith. Capital of charity. Capital of everything.

Capital also of glory (temporal). But what is glory, after all that.

Capital of lust (so it is said). Capital of vice (so it is claimed). Capital of virtue. Capital, apparently, capital of sin. City of so many grandeurs, of all grandeur. City of so much baseness, of all destitution. City of all charity, in all the meanings of this word, excellently, eminently, infinitely in this technical meaning which infinitely outweighs all the others. City of pride and humility, of modesty always. Capital of thought. Capital of the production and of the consumption of thought.

City in all the world where temporal "climbers" succeed the most, the quickest, the most infallibly, the most automatically. And all the temporal snobs. Also the city which wears out the temporal "climbers" the most infallibly and the most quickly and as it were automatically; and which, almost at once, breaks their backs, so that they need no more be mentioned.

City from which, alas, the greatest amount of intelligence radiates in the world.—Brain which elaborates the greatest amount of thought. Heart from which rises in all that mist visible from Montmartre, in that fog, in that marine vapor, in that industrial vapor, coal dust, dust from wooden pavings, dust from cobblestones, dust from leavings, filth of all kinds, dust of steam, water vapor, today's vapors of gasoline and petroleum and of so many heavy oils, vapors too of so many unhealthy exhalations... Heart from which rises past all this temporal mist, the greatest amount of specifically, the greatest amount of technically veritable prayer.

Joan of Arc

SHE WAS OF the people, and Christian, and saintly. She was most certainly in a sense a woman at arms. One might almost say a warrior. She was unquestionably a very great military leader.—She was a flower of the Christian race and of the French race, a flower of Christendom, a flower of all heroic virtues.—

Whatever may be the powers of the living springs, whatever may be the devices and the perpetual emission and effusion, whatever may be the inexhaustible innovations of grace, at the same time there indubitably exists a certain technique, a certain blessed hierarchic arrangement, as it were professional, a framework and a skeleton almost of the *métier*, a certain blessed professional hierarchy of heroic virtue and saintliness. There are degrees which are the very degrees of the Throne. To the first degree Joan of Arc possessed in their fullness the virtues of war, which are not small. I mean to say by that, very expressly and very properly, that she entered into the game of war and into the risk of war fully, without any restriction, without any intervention, without any interposition on the part of divine protection. She obeyed, she accomplished a divine mission proper in a human world without having felt a corresponding divine protection proper. She had received the commandment, she had received the vocation, she had received the mission. She obeyed, she carried out the commandment, she responded to the vocation, she accomplished her mission. She passed to the achievement, to the accomplishment of her mission in the midst of a hard (and tender) humanity, in a world, in a Christendom hard and tender, herself being gentle and firm, strong, gentle, sometimes apparently hard. Apparently harsh. During her whole mission she received assistance of counsel, this we know, through the constantly renewed, constantly present assistance and counsel of her voices. Through this sort of assistance of counsel, almost feudal, perpetually renewed, perpetually present. During her whole mission, and in this I include her captivity, in spite of the few absences that she had to suffer in its course and her death. During her whole mission, which extended into her captivity, she received constant assistance of counsel from her voices and an abundance of graces of which we can have no idea. The day of her death she received a grace which perhaps was never given similarly and to such an extent to any other saint, so that the day of her death already was no longer for her the last day of life on earth but literally, really, already the first day of her eternal life. But after all, with this mission, with this vocation, with all these graces, with all these gifts, with this constant presence of counsel, she never received either the grace, or the gift, or the counsel, or any privilege of being invulnerable. She waged war, exposed to all the accidents of war. She, like everybody else, waged a war like everybody else. Less fortunate than many saints, less fortunate than many prophets even, and than many rulers of the people of Israel, she did not find fighting beside her the angels who assisted her with their counsels, or the saints. Never have the words of Jesus—"Thinkest thou that I cannot now pray to my Father and He shall presently give me more than twelve legions of angels? But how then shall the Scriptures be fulfilled, that thus it must be?"—never have they been so fully accomplished in a saint, and here we meet again with this vocation, this unique election, this unique imitation by which one can say that of all the saints, she it was to whom certainly it was given that her life and her Passion and her death should most closely imitate the life and the Passion and the death of Jesus.—

Twelve legions of angels. She did not ask for them any more than He did. She never asked for them. This counsel, which she had, which was like the consequence, like the natural sequence of the commandment, of the vocation, like the natural sequence, supernatural and natural, coming from the same voices, borne by the same agency, this counsel which she had and had still, almost familiarly, so to speak, for her use as daily prayer, this habitual counsel like morning and evening prayer, she asked for often and asked for it again. Supernatural, direct, physical help in war, assistance in war, supernatural troops of war which she did not have, she never asked for.—

It would seem that never had the King of Heaven wished so expressly as in the person of this great saint that one of His daughters should win of herself the palms of martyrdom.

She knew it. Not only was she not protected, she was not ensured against sickness and against wounds and against military defeat, but she knew that she was not ensured against sickness and against wounds and against military defeat.

She accomplished a divine task through merely human means. She carried out a divine commandment through strictly human means. She responded to a divine vocation through exclusively human means, by a work, by a military war, by operations, by efforts strictly human. She accomplished a divine mission through simply human means. This is what gives her a place apart, a most eminent place in the hierarchy of sanctities. Let us also note, let us note further that the substance in which this sanctity had to be exerted was the most extraordinary, the farthest removed from the habitual order, one might almost say the most foreign to habitual substances of sanctity. And even that one most contrary and hostile to the habitual substances of sanctity. Among all saints she it was who was truly sent on a mission extraordinary. By these two commandments she has a unique place in the hierarchy of sanctities, she is holy and blessed among all saints while at the same time through the first commandment she is a woman among all the saints.

If on the other hand one wishes to consider her, no longer in her order of sanctity but in her order of humanity, who does not immediately perceive that in this order she is a unique woman? A unique being. For if one wishes, she is of the race of saints, and if one wishes, she is of the race of heroes. Coming from God and returning to God and constantly receiving assistance of counsel from her voices, in all her being she is a saint. She is of the race of saints. But in this hard humanity of the fifteenth century, and of all the centuries, accomplishing by purely human means such an array of purely human exploits in a purely human war, in all of this purely human action, through all her externally directed action, through her whole engagement of body and soul in military action, in an entire action of war, by her entire condition, by her entire active being she is a hero, she is of the race of heroes.

Now, not only are the race of heroes and the race of saints not identical, but they are two scarcely or ill-connected races. One might almost say that they do not care for each other, that they do not like to keep company together, that they are embarrassed to be in one another's company. There is something inexpressibly profound and which should be fathomed, through which the race of heroes and the race of saints stand in some inexpressibly deep contradiction. There are perhaps no two races of men that are so profoundly foreign one to the other, so far removed one from the other, so antithetical one to the other as are the race of heroes and the race of saints. Doubtless one would discover that this profound contradiction merely manifests, but under a form, perhaps under its sharpest form, under its eminent form, that eternal contradiction of the temporal and the eternal.

Now Joan of Arc, precisely because she exerted her saintliness in purely human trials, by purely human means, precisely because she had remained entirely vulnerable in battle, vulnerable to sickness, vulnerable to wounds, vulnerable to capture, vulnerable to death, vulnerable to defeat and to all defeat, fully exposed like an ancient hero to all warlike adventure, precisely for this reason she is of the race of heroes as she is of the race of saints. And as in the race of saints she is not only a saint among all saints and a woman among all saints, so in a parallel manner, so in the race of heroes, she is a hero among all heroes and a woman. She is not less eminent in the heroic hierarchy than in the sacred hierarchy. And thus she is at a point of intersection unique in the history of humanity. Two races meet in her that meet nowhere else. By a unique intersection of these two races, by an election, by a vocation unique in the history of the world she is at once saintly among all heroes, heroic among all the saints.

I DO NOT believe that I have ever spoken of the *Catholic world*. I have often spoken of the Church, of communion. I do not feel truly myself, I do not really touch the bottom of my thought save when I write Christendom. Only then I fully see what I say.

POETRY

A CURSE ON WAR

Joan of Arc Speaks

WHAT AVAIL OUR efforts of a day? What avail our charities? I really can't give all the time. I can't give all. I can't give to everyone. I really can't give the passers-by all my father's bread. And even if I did, would it make any difference? In the mass of the famished. (*She stops spinning by imperceptible degrees.*) For every wounded man we happen to look after, for every child we feed, indefatigable war makes hundreds of wounded, of sick and homeless people, every day. All our efforts are vain. War has more power than anything when it comes to making people suffer. Ah, a curse on war! And a curse on those who brought it to the land of France.

TRY AS WE may, try as we may, they will always go faster than we, they will always do more than we, a deal more than we. All that is needed to set a farm ablaze is a flint. It takes, it took years to build it. It isn't difficult. One doesn't have to be so clever. It takes months and months, it took work and more work to make the crop grow. And all that is needed to set a crop ablaze is a flint. It takes years and years to make a man grow, it took bread and more bread to feed him, and work and more work, and all kinds of work. And all that is needed to kill him is one blow. One sword thrust and it's done. To make a good Christian, the plow has to work twenty years. To kill a good Christian, the sword has to work one minute. It's always that way. It's like the plow to work twenty years and it's like the sword to work one minute. It's always that way. It's like the plow to work twenty years and it's like the sword to work one minute, and to do more, to be stronger, to make an end of things. So we people will always be the weaker ones. We will always go more slowly, we will always do less. We are the party of those who build up. They are the party of those who pull down. We are the party of the plow. They are the party of the sword. We will always be beaten. They will always get the better of us, on top of us.

No matter what we say.

For one wounded man dragging himself along the roads, for one man we pick up on the roads, for one child dragging himself along the roadsides, how many people are wounded, and sick, and forsaken, how many women are made unhappy and children forsaken because of the war, and how many are killed, and how many unfortunates lose their souls. Those who kill lose their souls because they kill. And those who are killed lose their souls because they are killed. Those who are strongest, those who kill lose their souls through the murder which they commit. And those who are killed, the man who is weaker, lose their souls through the murder which they suffer, for, seeing how weak they are and how bruised, always the same being weak, and the same unhappy, and the same beaten, and the same killed, then, unhappy ones, they despair of their salvation, because they despair of the goodness of God. Thus, no matter where one may turn, on both sides, it is a game in which, no matter how one plays or what one plays for, salvation is always bound to lose and perdition always bound to win. There is nothing but ingratitude, nothing but despair and perdition.

AND BREAD EVERLASTING. He who is too much in lack of daily bread no longer has any desire for bread everlasting, the bread of Jesus Christ.

CURSED BE WAR, cursed of God.

FRANCE MUST GO ON

Would the father's heart be in his work if he did not
  have his children,
If it weren't for his children?
And in winter when he is hard at work
In the forest,
When he works hardest
With his pruning hook and his saw and his axe and
  his hatchet,
In the icy forest,
In winter when the adders are asleep in the woods
  because they are frozen,
And when a bitter north wind blows,
Going through his bones,
Going clean through all his limbs,
And he is completely chilled and his teeth are likely to
  chatter,
And the frost puts icicles in his beard,
All of a sudden he thinks of his wife who has remained
  at home,
Of his wife who is such a good housekeeper,

Whose man he is before God,
And of his children who are quite peacefully staying at home,
Playing, having fun right now by the fireside,
Fighting perhaps,
Together,
For fun;
They pass before his eyes, in a flash before his memory's eyes, before the eyes of his soul,
They dwell in his memory and in his heart and in his soul and in the eyes of his soul,
They dwell in his gaze,
In a flash he sees his three children playing and laughing by the fireside.
His three children, two boys and a girl,
Whose father he is before God;
His eldest, his boy who was twelve in September,
His daughter who was nine in September,
And his youngest child who was seven in June,
Thus his daughter stands in the middle,
As it should be,
In order that she may be protected by her two brothers,
In this life,
One before and one after,
His three children who will succeed him and survive him
On earth,
Who will have his house and his land,
And should he own neither house nor land, will at least have his tools

(Should he own neither house nor land, they won't own
any either,
That is all)
(He managed to live without house and land,
They will do as he did. They will work)
His hatchet and his axe, and his pruning hook, and
his saw,
And his hammer, and his file,
And his shovel, and his pickaxe,
And his spade to dig the soil;
And should he own neither house nor land,
Should they not inherit his house and his land,
At any rate, they will inherit his tools,
Good tools,
The tools that he has used so many times,
That were accustomed to his hand,
That so often digged the same soil;
His tools, from being used so often, have made his hand
all callous and shiny,
But he, by using them so often, has made their handle
smooth and shiny,
And by dint of hard work, he now has a skin as hard
and as tanned as his tools' handles;
Through his tools' handles, his sons will find anew, his
sons will inherit the hardness of his hands,
But also their skill, their great skill,
Because he is a good plowman and a good woodcutter,
And a good winegrower;
And with his tools his sons will inherit, his children
will inherit

What he has given them, what no one could take away
  from them
(Not even God, almost)
(So much has God given to man),
The strength of his people, the strength of his blood;
For they came from him,
And they belong to France and to Lorraine,
Sons of a good people and of good stock.
Now good stock does not belie itself,
Good mother's sons;
And above all that which is above all, with his tools and
  his stock and his blood, his children will inherit
What is worth more than a house and a piece of land to
  leave to one's children,
For house and land are perishable and will perish,
And house and land are exposed to the winter wind,
To that bitter north wind that blows in that forest,
But God's blessing is blown by no wind;
What is worth more than tools, what is more
  hardworking, more workmanlike than tools,
What accomplishes more work than tools—
And tools end up by wearing out,
Like man,
What is worth more, what lasts longer than race and
  blood,
Even,
For the race itself and the blood are perishable and
  will perish,
Except the blood of Jesus
Which shall be shed for centuries and centuries,

And the race itself and the blood are exposed to the
  winter wind,
And perchance there is a winter for races,
With his house perchance, if he has one, and his land,
Surely with his tools and his race and his blood, his
  children will inherit
That which is above everything:
The blessing of God that is on his house and on his
  race,
The grace of God that is worth more than anything
(He knows it well),
That is on the poor man and on him who works
And who brings up his children properly,
He knows it well,
Because he promised it
And because he is supremely faithful in his promises.

His three children who are growing so fast,
Let us hope they don't fall ill,
And who will certainly be taller than he
(How proud he is of them in his heart),
And his two boys are going to be powerfully strong,
His two boys will replace him, his children will take his
  place on earth,
When he is no longer there,
His place in the parish and his place in the forest,
His place in church and his place at home,
His place in the market-town and his place in
  the vineyard,
And in the plain, and on the hillside, and in the valley,

His place in Christendom, don't you know,
His place as a man and his place as a Christian,
His place as a parishioner, his place as a plowman,
His place as a peasant,
His place as a father,
His place as a son of Lorraine and of France,
Because, good Lord, those are places which have to be kept,
And all that must go on,
When he is no longer there, just as it is going on now,
If not better;
Peasantry must go on,
And the wine and the wheat and the harvest and the vintage,
And the plowing of the soil,
And the feeding of the animals,
When he is no longer there, just as now,
If not better,
Christendom must go on,
The Church militant,
And for that there must be Christians,
Always;
The parish must go on,
France and Lorraine must go on
A long time after he is gone,
Just as well as at present,
If not better;
With tenderness he thinks of that time when he will no longer be there and when his children will have taken his place

On earth,
Before God,
Of that time when he will no longer be alive and when his children will live.
And when they mention his name in the market-town, when they talk about him, when his name is uttered, as conversation will have it, it won't be of him they will talk, but of his sons.
Altogether, it will be he and it won't be he, since it will be his sons;
It will be his name, and it will no longer be and it will not be his name since it will have become his sons' name;
And he is proud of that in his heart and how tenderly he thinks of it,
That he will no longer be himself but his two sons,
And that his name will no longer be his name but his sons' name;
That his name will no longer be at his service, but at his sons' service
Who will hear the name honestly before God,
Heads high, proudly,
Like him,
Better than he,
And when they say his name, it is his son they will be calling, it is his son they will mean.
As for him, he will long since have been in the graveyard
Around the church,
He, that is, his body,

Side by side with his fathers and the fathers of his
fathers,
Aligned with them,
With his father and his grandfather whom he knew,
And with all the others, all those he never knew,
All the men and all the women of his race,
All the ancient men and all the ancient women,
His ancestors and grandsires.
And grandams,
As many as there were since the parish was founded
By some holy founder
Who came from Jesus;
His body, for as regards his soul, it has been a long time
Since he commended it to God,
Placing it under the protection of his patron saints.

He will sleep, his body will thus be resting
Among his people (awaiting his people),
Awaiting the resurrection of the bodies;
Until the resurrection of the bodies, thus will his
body rest.

He thinks tenderly of the time when they will not
need him
And when things will have to go on just the same,
Because there will be others
Who will bear the same load
And who, perhaps, and who, no doubt, will bear
it better.

He thinks tenderly of the time when he will no
longer be,
Because, you know, a man can't live forever,
A man can't be and at the same time have been,
And when everything will go on just the same,
When everything will go on no worse,
On the contrary,
When everything will go on better,
On the contrary,
Because his children will be there, all right!

His children will do better than he, to be sure,
And the world will fare better,
Later on.
He feels no jealousy on that score,
On the contrary,
Nor because he himself came into the world in
sorry times
And doubtless prepared for his sons times perhaps
less sorry.
What crazy fellow would be jealous of his sons and
of his son's sons?

He is working only for his children, is he not?
He thinks tenderly of the time when he will no longer
be much thought of, except because of his children,
(If only he is thought of sometimes; seldom);
When his name echoes (cordially) in the market-town,
It will be because someone calls his son Marcel or his
son Pierre,

It will be because someone needs his son Marcel or his son Pierre,
And that man will call them, and will be happy to see them, and will go look for them,
Because they will reign then and bear the name,
They will reign with the men of their age and of their time,
They will reign on the face of the earth;
Perhaps for some time still an old fellow will remember
And say:
"The two Sévin lads, they are good lads.
It's not surprising."
They have someone to take after.
"Their father was such a good man."
And for some time, the young people will repeat confidently:
"The old man was such a good man."
But already they won't know anything about it; even that remark will cease to be heard
Then they won't know any more, and even that, even those words will be silent
He thinks tenderly of the time when he won't even be a remark;
That is what he is working at, that is what he is working for.
Indeed, isn't it for his children that a man works?
He won't be any more than a body in six feet of earth, under six feet of earth, under a cross.
But his children will be living.

He greets with tenderness the new times when he will
be no more,
When he will not be,
When his children will be,
His children's reign.
He thinks tenderly of that time which will no longer be
his time,
But his children's time,
The reign (in time) of his children on earth.
At that time, when people say *the Sévins*, they will not
mean him, but them,
No more, with no explanation.

His children will bear that name of Sévin,
(Or that name of Chénin, or that name of Jouffin, or
Damrémont or any other name of Lorraine,
Any other name, Christian, French, or of Lorraine).

At the thought of his children who will have grown
into men and women,
At the thought of his children's time, or his children's
reign
On earth,
In their turn,
A tenderness, a warmth, a feeling of pride rise
up within him
(Lord, may not that be vainglory? But God will
forgive him).
God of justice, how valiant will his sons be in
the forest,

Lads as strong as oaks,
In the forest where the winter north wind blows,
The bitter north wind
That will go through their bones
And put icicles in their beards.

He laughs when he thinks how funny they will look,
He laughs within himself and perhaps even on
the surface,
Outwardly.

When he thinks how they will look when they will
have a beard.

And he thinks tenderly of his daughter who will be
such a good housekeeper,
Because she will be like her mother.
As for him, he won't be living any more, that is
understood,
He will have lost his taste for bread,[1]
But there will be others, just God, there will be others,
We must hope so,
Who already have a taste for bread and who will know
how to bite into a fine loaf of bread,
Who will eat with a hearty appetite
Their daily bread,
Who will heartily eat their daily bread and their
bread eternal,

---

1. *Perdre le goût du pain*, a French idiom meaning *to die.*

(They will very easily do without him, and he will no longer be seated at the table, because you have to squeeze around the table when newcomers arrive and push),
Others, his children, who will live and die after him if all turns out as it should,
And whom he will see again in heaven.

There will be others, thank God:
France must go on.

MORTAL SIN AND LEPROSY

This poem is based on a passage from Joinville's History of Saint Louis. *The king of France and his baron Joinville were talking one day of leprosy, not an uncommon subject in thirteenth-century conversations, and Joinville declared that his horror of that disease was such that he would prefer committing thirty mortal sins rather than become a leper. Whereupon Saint Louis gently reproved him and said that it were better to be a leper than to commit one mortal sin. This is what God the Father has to say on the subject.*

God Speaks

Having once known what it is to be loved freely, one no longer finds any flavor in submissions.
When one has known what it means to be loved by free men, the prostrations of slaves no longer please.

When one has seen Saint Louis on his knees, one no longer wishes to see
Those Oriental slaves lying prone on the ground
At body's length, on their stomachs, on the ground. To be loved freely,
Nothing weighs as much as that weighty thing, nothing weighs as much as that thing of great price,
It is certainly my greatest invention.
Once one has tasted,
What it is to be loved freely
All the rest is no more than submissions.
That is why, says God, we are so fond of those Frenchmen,
And why, among all other people, we love them in an un-paralleled way,
And why they will always be my eldest sons.
They have freedom in their blood.
Everything they do, they do freely.
They are less slavish and freer in sin itself
Than the others in their exercises. Through them we have tasted,
Through them we have invented, through them we have created
This thing: to be loved by free men. When Saint Louis says that he loves me,
I know that he loves me,
At least I know that that one loves me, because he is a French baron. Through them we have known
What it is to be loved by free men. All the prostrations in the world

Are not worth the beautiful upright kneeling of a free man. All the submissions, all the self-abasements in the world
Are not worth a beautiful prayer, an upright, kneeling prayer of those free men. All the submissions in the world
Are not worth the soaring point
The beautiful straight soaring of a single invocation
Of a free love. When Saint Louis loves me, says God, I am sure,
I know what is meant. He is a free man, he is a free baron of the Ile de France. When Saint Louis loves me
I am aware, I know what it is to be loved.
(Now that is everything). No doubt he fears God,
But with a noble fear, all filled, all swollen,
All replete with love, like a fruit swollen with juice.
In no wise a cowardly, a base fear, a nasty funk
Which claws at the stomach, but a great, but a lofty, but a noble fear,
The fear of displeasing me, because he loves me, and of disobeying me, because he loves me.
And because he loves me, the fear
Of not being found agreeable
And loving and loved under my gaze. No infiltration in that noble fear,
Of an evil funk and of a pernicious and vile cowardice.
And when he loves me, it is true. And when he says that he loves me, it is true. And when he says that he would prefer
To be a leper than to fall into mortal sin (so much does

he love me), it is true.
When he says it, I know it is true.
It isn't only true that he says it. It is true because it is true. He doesn't say it because it sounds well.
He doesn't say that because he saw it in books nor because someone told him to say it. He says it because it is so.
He loves me to that extent. He loves me thus. Freely. A proof of it I have in the same race
And that is the Sire de Joinville (whom I love so very much, just the same), another French baron,
Who would on the contrary have committed thirty mortal sins rather than become a leper.
(Thirty, poor man, how little he knows what he is talking about.)
Doesn't mind saying what he thinks,
That is, saying the opposite
In the presence of even so great a king
And of so great a saint
Whom he nevertheless knew to be such,
That is, displeasing such a great king and such a great saint.
The freedom of speech
Of one who doesn't wish to run the risk.
Of being a leper rather than falling into mortal sin,
Insures for me the freedom of speech of him who prefers being a leper
To falling into mortal sin.
If one says what he thinks, the other too says what he thinks.

One proves the other...
In their rigmarole about leprosy and mortal sin, this is how I figure, says God.
When Joinville had rather have committed thirty mortal sins than to be a leper,
And when Saint Louis had rather be a leper than to fall into one single mortal sin,
I do not conclude, says God, that Saint Louis loves me in an ordinary way
And that Joinville loves me thirty times less than the ordinary way,
That Saint Louis loves me according to measure, in just the wanted measure,
And that Joinville loves me thirty times less than the measure.
I reckon, on the contrary, says God, this is how I figure, this is how I conclude.
I conclude, on the contrary, that Joinville loves me in the ordinary way,
Honestly, just as a poor man is capable of loving me,
Must love me;
And that Saint Louis, on the contrary, loves me thirty times above the ordinary,
Thirty times more than honorably;
That Joinville loves me according to measure,
And that Saint Louis loves me thirty times more than according to measure
(And if I put that one in my heaven, at least I know why).
That is how I reckon, says God. And so my reckoning is

fair, because that leprosy which they had in mind,
That leprosy of which they talked, and about being a leper,
Was anything but an imaginary leprosy and a make-believe leprosy and an exercise leprosy,
It wasn't a leprosy which they had seen in books and heard talked about
More or less vaguely,
It wasn't a leprosy to talk about, nor a leprosy to frighten people in conversation and in figures of speech,
But this was the real leprosy, and they talked about having it themselves, in very sooth,
They knew it well, they had seen it twenty times
In France and in Holy Land,
That disgusting mealy disease, that filthy itch, that evil mange,
That repellent scabby disease which makes man
The horror and shame of man,
That ulcer, that dry rot, in a word that definitive leprosy
Which eats into the skin and the face and the arm and the hand
And the thigh and the leg and the foot
And the stomach and the skin and the bones and the nerves and the veins,
That dry white mold which spreads little by little
And bites as if with a mouse's teeth,
And makes a man the refuse and the flight of man,
And destroys a body like a granulous mold,
And grows on the body those awful white lips,
Those awful dry lips of wounds,

And which always advances and never draws back,
And always wins and never loses,
And goes to the end,
And makes of a man a walking corpse.
It was that leprosy they were talking about and of none
other.
It was that leprosy they had in mind and none other,
A real leprosy, in no way a leprosy of exercise.
It was that leprosy which he preferred to have, none other.
Well, I think it is thirty times more startling
And that it means loving me thirty times and that it
means thirty times love.

Ah, to be sure, if Joinville with the eyes of the soul
had seen
What manner of thing is that leprosy of the soul
Which we not in vain call mortal sin,
If with the eyes of the soul he had seen
That dry rot of the soul infinitely more evil,
Infinitely more ugly, infinitely more pernicious,
Infinitely more malignant, infinitely more odious,
He himself would immediately have understood how
absurd his remark was,
And that the question cannot be raised. But all do not
see with the eyes of the soul.
I understand that, says God. All are not saints, such is
my Christendom.
There are sinners too, there have to be some, it is thus.
He was a good Christian, nevertheless, all in all, he was
a sinner, there have to be some in Christendom.

He was a good Frenchman, Jean, sire de Joinville, a baron of Saint Louis! At least he spoke his mind.
Those people make up the bulk of the army. There have to be troops.
It is not sufficient to have leaders who march ahead.
Those people start most honestly on a crusade, at least once every other time, and very honestly go on a crusade,
They fight very well and are very properly killed and win the kingdom of Heaven
Just like any other kingdom…
But there you are, they think: I have only one body
(Fools, they forget the principal thing,
They forget not only the soul but the body of their eternity,
The body of the resurrection of the bodies),
Only one body have I, they think (thinking only of their earthly body);
If that nasty leprosy takes hold of me, I am lost.
(They mean that their temporal body is temporally lost…)
Now they cling to their body. One would think that they believed it was the only thing they had.
Yet they know that they have a soul. Life is the union of soul and body.
Death lies in their sundering. But their body seems to them
A strong and jolly fellow.
They are under the impression that leprosy will annihilate their whole body and that it will hold

them unto the end (they do not consider that at
the end of that end begins the real beginning),
And so they would prefer to have something else
than leprosy.
I suppose they would prefer to catch
A disease of their liking.
It is always the same business.
They don't mind facing the most terrible ordeals
And offering me the most awe-inspiring exercises,
So long as they themselves have beforehand
Chosen them. Thereupon the Pharisees cry out and
exclaim
And shout and make faces, and those execrable
Pharisees
Above all pray, saying: Lord, we thank Thee.
That Thou hast not made us like unto that man
Who feareth to catch leprosy. Now I say, on the
contrary, says God,
I myself do say: it is something to catch leprosy.
I know what leprosy is; I made it.
I know it. I say: it is something to catch leprosy.
Nor did I ever say that the ordeals and the exercises of
their lives,
And the diseases and the miseries of their lives,
And the distresses of their lives were nothing.
I have always said, on the contrary, and I have always
thought
And I have always weighed that it was something,
And indeed it must be believed that it was something
Since my Son performed so many miracles on the sick

And since I gave the king of France the power
To heal the king's evil.
The Pharisees raise a hue and cry over the one who doesn't want to catch leprosy,
And they are scandalized, those virtuous ones.
But I who am not virtuous,
Says God,
I do not shout neither am I scandalized.

I do not figure, I do not conclude that that Joinville is thirty times below the ordinary.
But I conclude, but I figure, on the contrary,
That it is that Saint Louis who is out of the ordinary, thirty times out of the ordinary, thirty times extraordinary, thirty times above the ordinary.

I do not figure, I do not conclude
That Joinville is thirty times a coward.
But on the contrary, I conclude and I figure:
That it is that Saint Louis who is brave thirty times,
Brave thirty times above the ordinary and more than the measure.

I do not figure, I do not conclude
That Joinville is thirty times lower,
But on the contrary I conclude and I figure:
That it is that Saint Louis who is thirty times higher,
Thirty times high above the ordinary and more than the measure.

I do not figure, I do not conclude
That Joinville is thirty times small,
But I just know that he is a man.
And on the contrary I conclude and I figure,
This is how I figure,
And it is so.
I conclude and I figure that it is that Saint Louis, king of France,
Who is thirty times great, thirty times above the ordinary and more than the measure.

And who is thirty times close to my heart and thirty times my son's brother.
The Pharisees raise a hue and cry over the one who does not wish to catch leprosy,
But the saint does not raise a hue and cry and is not scandalized.
He knows human nature too well, and man's infirmity, and he is only profoundly grieved.

The Pharisees raise a hue and cry over that man who does not wish to catch leprosy.
See on the contrary how gently the Saint speaks to him,
Firmly but gently.
And that firmness is all the more sure and gives me all the more certainty, all the more assurance and all the more guarantee since it is gentle.
The hearts of sinners are not taken by violence.

They are not pure enough. Only the kingdom of heaven is taken by violence.

HOPE

I am, says God, Master of the Three Virtues.

Faith is a faithful wife.
Charity is an ardent mother.
But hope is a tiny girl.

I am, says God, the Master of Virtues.

Faith is she who remains steadfast during centuries
and centuries.
Charity is she who gives herself during centuries
and centuries.
But my little hope is she
Who rises every morning.

I am, says God, the Lord of Virtues.

Faith is she who remains tense during centuries
and centuries.

Charity is she who unbends during centuries
and centuries.
But my little hope
Is she who every morning
Wishes us good day.

I am, says God, the Lord of Virtues.

Faith is a soldier, a captain holding a fort,
One of the king's cities,
In the borderland of Gascony, in the borderland
of Lorraine.
Charity is a physician, a little sister of the poor,
Who nurses the sick, who nurses the wounded,
The king's poor,
In the borderland of Gascony, in the borderland of
Lorraine.
But my little hope is she
Who says how do you do to the poor and to
the orphan.

I am, says God, the Lord of Virtues.

Faith is a church, a cathedral rooted in the soil
of France.
Charity is a hospital, an almshouse which gathers up all
the miseries of the world.
But if it weren't for hope, all that would be nothing but
a cemetery.

I am, says God, the Lord of Virtues.

Faith is she who watches during centuries
  and centuries.
Charity is she who watches during centuries
  and centuries.
But my little hope is she
Who goes to bed every night
And gets up every morning
And really sleeps very well.

I am, says God, the Lord of that virtue.

My little hope is she who goes to sleep every night,
In that child's crib of hers,
After having said her prayers properly,
And who every morning wakes up and rises
And says her prayers with a new look in her eyes.

I am, says God, Lord of the Three Virtues.

Faith is a great tree, an oak rooted in the heart of France.
And under the wings of that tree, Charity, my daughter
  Charity shelters all the woes of the world.
And my little hope is nothing but that little earnest of a
  bud which shows itself at the beginning of April.

And when one sees the tree, when one looks at the oak,
That rough bark of the oak thirteen and fourteen
  hundred years old,

Which will be a centenarian and centuries old for centuries and centuries,
That hard, rough bark and those limbs which are like a confusion of huge arms
(A confusion which is an order),
And those roots which thrust into the soil and lay hold of it like a confusion of huge legs
(A confusion which is an order),
When one sees such strength and such roughness, the tender little bud no longer seems to be anything at all.
It is the bud that looks as if it were the tree's parasite, as if it ate at the tree's table,
Like mistletoe, like a mushroom.

It is the bud that looks as if it were getting nourishment from the tree (indeed the peasant calls them *greedies*), it is the bud that looks as if it were resting on the tree, coming out of the tree, as if it could not be, as if it could not exist without the tree. And today, in truth, it comes out of the tree, at the armpit of the limbs, at the armpit of the leaves, and it can no longer exist without the tree. It looks as if it came from the tree, as if it were robbing the tree of its sustenance.
And yet it is from that bud, on the contrary, that everything comes. Without a bud that once appeared, the tree would not exist. Without those thousands of buds that come out once at the beginning of April and sometimes in the last days of March, nothing would last, the tree would not last and would not keep its place as a tree (that place must be kept), without that sap which

rises and weeps in the month of May, without those thousands of buds that begin to grow tenderly at the armpits of the hard limbs.

Every place must be kept. All life comes from tenderness. All life comes from that tender, delicate April bud and from that sap that weeps in May, and from the cotton wool and the down of that delicate white bud that is clad, that is warmly, that is tenderly protected by the tuft of the fleece of a vegetable wool, the wool of a tree. In that cotton-like tuft lies the secret of all life. The rough bark looks like a cuirass in comparison with that tender bud. But the rough bark is nothing but a hardened bud, a bud grown old. And that is why the tender bud always pierces through, always springs up from under the rough bark.

The toughest warrior was once upon a time a tender child, a child fed on milk; and the most rugged martyr, the toughest martyr on the wooden horse, the martyr with the most rugged bark, with the roughest skin, the hardest martyr clawed by talons and nails, was once upon a time a tender child, a child fed on milk.

Without that bud which does not look like anything, which seems as nothing, all that would be as dead wood.

And the dead wood will be cast into the fire.

Now I tell you, says God, that without that late April budding, without those thousands of buds, without that one little budding of hope, which obviously anyone can break off, without that tender, cotton-like bud,

which the first man who comes along can snap off with his nail, the whole of my creation would be nothing but dead wood.
And the dead wood will be cast into the fire.

And my whole creation would be nothing than a huge cemetery.
Now my son has told them: *Let the dead bury their dead.*

Alas my son, alas my son, alas my son;
My son who, on the cross, had a skin as dry as dry bark;
A withered skin, a wrinkled skin, a tanned skin;
A skin that was split by the nails;
My son had been a tender child, a child fed on milk,
A childhood, a budding, a promise, a pledge;
An attempt, an origin; the beginning of a redeemer;
A hope of salvation, a hope of redemption.

O day, O evening, O night of the burial,
Fall of that night which I shall never see again,
O night so dear to the heart by what you accomplish
And because you are as soothing as balsam,
Night on that mountain and in that valley,
O night, I have so often said that I should not see you again,
O night, I shall see you in my eternity.
My will be done. O that time it was that my will was done.
Night, I see you still. Three great gallows went up, and

my son in the middle.
A hill, a valley. They had gone up from that city which I had given to my people. They had gone up.
My son between those two thieves. One wound in his side. Two wounds in his hands. Two wounds in his feet. Wounds on his forehead.
Women who wept as they stood. And that leaning head, bowed upon his breast.
And that poor dirty beard, all sullied with dust and blood,
That red beard with two points,
And that sullied hair, all disordered, which I would have kissed so often,
That beautiful red hair, still wet with blood from the crown of thorns,
All sullied, all clotted with blood. All was fulfilled.
He had borne too much.
That head which leaned forward, which I should have placed on my breast,
That shoulder which I should have placed against my shoulder,
And that heart no longer beating which had so long beaten with love.
Three or four women who wept as they stood. As for the men, I don't remember, I don't think there were any more.
Perhaps they had thought it was too much of a climb.
All was over. All was consummated. It was the end.
And the soldiers went away, and in their rounded shoulders they carried away the Roman might.

It was then, O Night, that you came.
O night, the same
The same that comes every evening and that had come so many times since the primeval darkness,
The same that descended on Abel's smoking altar and on Abel's dead body, on that mangled body, on the first murder committed in the world.
O selfsame night, you descended on the lacerated body, on the first, on the greatest murder in the world. It was then, O night, that you came.
The same that had descended on so many crimes since the beginning of the world,
And on so many stains and on so much bitterness,
And on that sea of ingratitude, you were the same that descended on my grief.
And on that hill and in that valley of my desolation, it was then, O night, that you came.
O night, will it then have to be, will it have to be that my paradise
Be nought but a great transparent night falling on the sins of the world?
Will it be thus, O night, that you will come?
It was then, O night, that you came, and you alone were able to finish, you alone were able to fulfill that day among days.
Just as you fulfilled that day, O night, you will fulfill the world,
And my paradise will be a great luminous night,
And all I shall have to offer
In my offering, I too, in my offertory,

SAINTS AND SINNERS

To so many martyrs and to so many tortioners,
To so many souls and to so many bodies,
To so many undefiled and to so many who are defiled,
To so many sinners and to so many saints,
To so many faithful and to so many penitents,
And to so many sorrows, and to so many bereavements,
  and to so many tears, and to so many wounds,
And to so much blood,
And to so many hearts that have beaten so long
With love, with hatred,
And to so many hearts that have bled so long
With love, with hatred,
Shall it be said that it must be,
And that I shall perforce have to offer,
And that they will not ask any more than that,
That they will desire no more than that,
That they will not relish anything else but that,
On those stains and on so much bitterness,
And on that boundless sea of ingratitude
The slow descending of a night eternal.

O night, you did not have to go and ask Pilate's
  permission. That is why I love and greet you,
And glorify you among all, and among all you
  glorify me,
And do me honor and glory...

I am, says God, the Lord of Virtues.
Faith is the sanctuary lamp
That burns forever.

Charity is that big, beautiful log fire
That you light in your hearth
So that my children the poor may come and warm themselves before it on winter evenings.
And all around Faith, I see all my faithful
Kneeling together in the same attitude, and with one voice
Uttering the same prayer.
And around Charity, I see all my poor
Sitting in a circle around that fire
And holding out their palms to the heat of the hearth.
But my hope is the bloom, and the fruit, and the leaf, and the limb,
And the twig, and the shoot, and the seed, and the bud.
Hope is the shoot, and the bud of the bloom
Of eternity itself.

THE HOLY INNOCENTS

The theme of this poem is that beautiful old hymn by Prudentius: Salvete Flores Martyrum, *or rather it is a commentary on a few lines from that hymn, the commentary being made with tenderness and humor by God the Father.*

Nemo poterat dicere canticum, nisi illa centum quadraginta quatuor millia, qui empti sunt de terra.
"No man could learn that song but the hundred and forty and four thousand, which were redeemed from the earth" (Rev. 14:3).

Qui empti sunt de terra. So many others died in my
Son's name,
In nomine Patris, et Filii, et Spiritus Sancti.
So many died to preserve the honor
Of my Son's name; and they
Who are alone to hear that name on their foreheads
And alone can sing that new song,
Are assuredly the only ones on earth;
To whom my Son's name was totally unknown. Such is

my decree.
That name for which they died, they did not know,
They never knew it on earth. That is what I like, says God.
Now, perhaps, they know it.
Forever and ever, it can be read
On one hundred and forty-four thousand foreheads.
On none other.
On not one more. But when they were alive and on earth,
One can say that they never knew what people were talking about,
Nor even that people were talking, nor that one could talk (about something). That is what pleases me, says God.
Now, they were crying, and laughing, and sucking, and screaming, and sleeping.
It was their great, it was their most serious occupation.
And a day came
When,
A day (they did not know the name of Herod anymore than that of Jesus)
(And they did not know the name of Jesus anymore than that of Herod. I shall venture to say
That they were equally indifferent to both those names.)
Now both those men,
Jesus, Herod—Herod, Jesus,
Antagonists, were simply going to obtain for them
The glory of my paradise,
The kingdom of heaven and eternal glory.

A day came
When a horde of soldier brutes, attending to their
  business
(But exceeding a little its limits, all the same),
An onrush of brutes went by, gendarmes of a kind,
  ogres as in fairy tales, bogey men for children,
Carrying sabers that were like big cutlasses,
And they were Herod's soldiers.
An onrush, a tumult. An uproar; arms with sleeves
  rolled up, an outcry.
Shrieks. Teeth. Glistening looks.
Women fleeing, women biting,
Just as they always do when they are not the strongest;
And there was nothing in the blood and the milk
But a great strewing of dead bodies,
A cemetery of babes and of young Jewish women.
You know, says God, what we have done with them.
Those eyes that had hardly opened to the light of the
  carnal sun,
Forever and ever were shut to the light of the
  carnal sun;
Those eyes that had hardly opened to the light of
  the earthly sun
Forever and ever were closed to the light of the
  earthly sun;
Those eyes that had hardly opened to the light of the
  temporal sun
Forever and ever were closed to the light of the
  temporal sun;
Those gazes that had hardly ascended towards the day

and the sun of time
Forever and ever were closed to those transient,
To those perishable lights.
Those voices, those lips that had never sung the praises of God on earth,
That had never opened but to ask to suck (but so does it suit me, says God),
Are thus the only ones, are today the only ones,
Are also the only ones that can sing that new song.
Qui empti sunt de terra. You see what we have done with them, says God.
Let the Innocents' hands be filled. Here is a case in point.
These Innocents had simply picked up in the scuffle
The kingdom of God and eternal life. What matter today
Their white limbs broken in the market-towns of Judea,
And their little dimpled arms cut off as by men pruning,
And their little fingers stiff and clenched in the palms of their hands,
And their cries thrust back into their throats, the criminal hands thrusting them back, hands crammed in their throats like a stopper, like a plug,
And the youthful blood gushing from the heart. What matter the severed limbs,
The white thighs like kid's flesh and like the tender thighs of little sucking pigs,
And their mothers shrieking like lunatics and biting the soldiers' wrists? As in a battle, after the battle
The prowlers, the robbers come and rifle the wounded

and the dead and the dying to take away and steal all that is worthwhile.
All that is worth something, novel prowlers, novel thieves, those innocents
In that battle, after that battle, rifled themselves
And in the clangor of arms, in the tumult and among the shrieks,
In the maddened galloping, in the frenzied pursuit, among the women felled to the ground, they snatched up all that counts,
They stole all that was worth something, for they plundered
Like those who rob corpses and they robbed themselves, and what they snatched up in the scuffle was no less
Than the kingdom of heaven and eternal life. *Hi empti sunt ex hominibus.* They alone,
Who alone perhaps on earth not only had never sung the praises of God,
But had never pronounced even my name nor my son's name,
They too, only they do not have at the corners of their mouths that ineffaceable line,
That line of misfortune and ingratitude
And of a bitterness that can never be satiated…

Undefiled in the way, thus did John see them,
Upon Mount Zion
Around the standing Lamb.
Everything seems to be for them. *They follow the Lamb*

whithersoever He goeth.
(The greatest saints, apparently, do not follow him everywhere.)

These were redeemed from among men:
(*From among men, from the midst of men, from being men*)
The greatest saints have been men, have not been redeemed from being men.

and in their mouth was found no lie:

for they are spotless before the throne of God.

And the Apostle calls them *primitiae Deo, et Agno*: *first-fruits to God, and to the Lamb*. That is to say, the first-fruits of the earth that are offered to God and to the Lamb. The other saints are the ordinary fruits, the fruits of the season. But they are the fruits
Of the very promise of the season.

And following the Apostle, the Church repeats: *Innocentes pro Christo infants occisi sunt,*

the Innocents for Christ
as children were massacred,

(*infantes*, very young children, very small children not yet able to speak)

ab iniquo rege
lactentes interfecti sunt:

by a wicked King
they, sucklings, were massacred:

(*lactentes*, full of milk, milky, at the age of milk, being yet on the milk diet,
fed on milk)

ipsum sequuntur Agnum sine macula;
they follow the Lamb himself spotless

(And such is the text, my child, that it is at the same time the Lamb that is spotless
And they with him who are spotless).

But the Church goes further, the Church goes beyond, the Church outstrips the Apostle.

No longer does the Church only say that they are the first fruits to God and to the Lamb,
But the Church invokes them and calls them

flowers of the Martyrs.

Literally meaning by those words that the other martyrs are the fruits, whereas these, among martyrs, are the flowers themselves.

Salvete FLORES *martyrum*:

Hail FLOWERS *of Martyrs.*

Laid out on the wooden horse, tied to the wooden
horse like fruit tied to an espalier,
The other martyrs, twenty centuries of martyrs,
Centuries of centuries of martyrs,
Are literally the fruits of the season,
Of each season arranged at intervals on the espalier,
And specially the autumn fruits;
And my son himself was gathered
In his three and thirtieth season. But they, those simple
innocents,
They are before the fruits, themselves, they are the
promise of the fruit.
Salvete flores Martyrum, those children less than two
years old are the flowers of all the other martyrs,
That is to say, the flowers that produce the other
martyrs.
At the very beginning of April, they are the rosy
blossom of the peach tree.
In mid-April, at the very beginning of May, they are the
white blossom of the pear tree.
In mid-May, they are the red blossom of the apple tree,
White and red.
They are the blossom itself and the bud of the blossom
and the down on the bud.
They are the bourgeon on the twig and the bud of the
blossom.

They are the pride of April and its sweet hope,
They are the pride of the woods and of the months,
They are little childhood.
The *Reminiscere* Sunday is only for them, because they remember.
The *Oculi* Sunday is only for them, because they see.
The *Laetare* Sunday is only for them, because they rejoice.
Passion Sunday is only for them, because they were the first Passion.
Palm Sunday is only for them, because they are the palm itself that bore much fruit.
And Easter Sunday is only for them, because they are risen again.
They are the flower of the hawthorn that blooms during Holy Week.
They are the flower of the blackthorn that blooms five weeks earlier.
They are the flower of all those plants and of all those rosaceous trees.
Promise of so many martyrs, they are rosebuds in a dew of blood.[2]
Salvete flores Martyrum,
Hail, flowers of Martyrs.

quos, lucis ipso in limine,
Christi insecutor sustulit,

2. An untranslatable pun on *rose* and *rosée* (dew). The numerous puns in Péguy's poems have well nigh driven the translator to despair.

ceu turbo nascentes rosas.

whom, on the very threshold, of light,
Christ's persecutor took away
(carried away)

ceu turbo nascentes rosas.

as a tempest with budding roses,
(That is, as the tempest, as a tempest takes away, carries away budding roses)

Vos prima Christi victima,
Grex immolatorum tener,
Aram sub ipsam simplices
Palma et coronis luditis.

Ye, first victim of Christ,
Tender flock of innocents slain
At the foot of the altar itself, simple
Simplices, simple souls, simple children,
Palma et coronis luditis. You play with the palm and the crowns. With your palm and your crowns.

Such is my paradise, says God. My paradise is just as simple as possible.
Nothing is so bare as my paradise.
Aram sub ipsam at the foot of the altar itself
These simple children *play* with their palms and with their martyrs' crowns.

That is what goes on in my paradise. What game can
one play
With a palm and with martyrs' crowns?
I suppose they roll hoops, says God, and perhaps they
play at "graces"[3]
(That is, I think so, for you must not believe that they
ever ask me for my permission),
And the evergreen palm apparently serves as a stick.

3. It is very characteristic of Péguy to end the third of his *Mysteries* with a pun; he could never resist a play on words. Here the reference is to a game played in France forty or fifty years ago. It was called *jeu de grâces* and required two sticks about the length of drumsticks, one small hoop and the ability to throw the hoop towards the sky with the help of the sticks and catch it again. Ladies excelled at this and their attitudes, when correct, were deemed worthy of the Graces. Hence the name, I suppose.

NIGHT

This poem might be described as one of the greatest moments of contemporary French poetry, and indeed of all French poetry. Péguy is here at his best. He is now a complete master of the language, that is, not content with obeying its laws, he compels it to follow him in all the intricacies of his thought and to express what, I believe, had never been said before him. He has subdued it as the magician in the Arabian Nights *subdues a genie. Péguy's French is so intensely his own that no one can use it after him without openly declaring himself a thief. There is much to be said about Péguy's grammar. At times, it is peculiar, I do not mean that it is uncertain. Péguy knew all the vast resources of grammar. He knew his grammar as only a Frenchman knows it who has studied Latin, French being little else than Latin continued, as Remy de Gourmont called it, Latin brought into Gaul by soldiers and merchants and thriving there until it became not another tongue, but Latin of another time. Quite often, however, Péguy's grammar goes wild, just as Blake's went wild, under the pressure of inspiration, and his syntax seems simply to burst asunder. He insists on the language saying things it has never said, and the language obeys, not without some awful stutterings. An example of this is the expression* POUR TOUJOURA, *which means, simply: forever. But* FOREVER, *in the mouth of God the Father, does not seem adequate to Péguy. He wants more eternity in that phrase, so, instead of saying* FOREVER, *God the Father says, in spite of grammar, in spite of usage, in spite of generations of professors:* FOR ETERNALLY.

Another of Péguy's characteristics is his inordinate love of puns. Not puns as jokes, not puns in the childlike manner of Charles Lamb, but serious puns, almost sacred puns. There are many such puns in the poem on night. Some have almost disappeared in the translation, but they never mar the beauty of the poem. Péguy who did everything in all seriousness, Péguy who proudly asserted that there was not one mortal sin in any of his books, Péguy raised the pun to a level which it had almost never known; I say ALMOST *because there is in the Gospels a most solemn and fundamental play on words.*

God Speaks

Nights follow each other and are linked, and for the child nights are continuous and are the innermost part of his very being.
Therein does he fall back. They are the innermost part of his life,

They are his very being. Night is the place, night is the being wherein he bathes, and is nourished, and is created, and is made,
Wherein he accomplishes his being,
Wherein he recovers his strength.
Night is the place, night is the being wherein he rests, wherein he retires, wherein he collects himself,
Wherein he enters again. And he comes out refreshed. Night is my most beautiful creation.
Now why doesn't man make use of it. I am told that there are men who don't sleep at night.
Night, for my children and for my young
Hope, is what it really is. It is the children who see and who know. It is my young hope
Who sees and who knows. Who knows what being means,
What the being called night is. Night it is that continues.
Children know very well. Children see very well.
And it is the days that are discontinuous. It is the days that pierce, that disrupt night,
And in no wise the nights that interrupt day.
It is day that troubles night with its noise,
Otherwise night would sleep.
And the solitude, and the silence of night is so beautiful and so great,
That it surrounds and corners and buries the days themselves,
That it makes an august enclosure around the restlessness of days.

Children are right, my little hope is right. All nights together
Meet and join as in a beautiful roundelay, as in a beautiful dance,
A dance of nights holding each other by the hand, whereas lean days
Make nothing more than a procession in which hands are not joined.
Children are right, my little Hope is right. Nights all together
Meet and join above the borders of days, hold out their hands to each other
Above the days, form a chain and more than a chain,
A roundelay, a dance, nights grasp each other's hands
Above the day, from morn till eve,
From the border of morn to the border of eve, leaning one towards the other,
The one coming down from the preceding day, leans back;
The one going up
To the next day,
Leans forward,
And both join, join hands,
Join their silence and their shadow,
And their piety and their august solitude,
Above the difficult borders,
Above the borders of hardworking day.
And all together, thus holding hands,
Overlapping the borders, wrists tied
To wrists, all the nights, one after another,

Together constitute night, and the days, one after
another,
Together do not constitute day. For they are nought but
lean days
That do not join hands. Now, just as life,
Earthly life,
In a big, general way (if I may say), is only a passage
between two borders,
An opening between the night before and the night
after,
A day,
An opening between the night of darkness and the
night of light,
So, in a small way, each day is only an opening.
A day.
Not only between the night before and the night after,
Between the borders,
But as children see it, as children sense it, and my
young Hope too, just as children know it,
In the night, in one and the same,
In one and the same night,
Where being recruits itself,
Deep in the night,
It is night that is continuous, wherein being recruits itself,
it is night that forms one long, continuous texture,
An endless continuous texture wherein days are
nothing but days,[4]

4. A play on *jour* meaning an aperture in an open-work stuff and *jour* meaning day.

Opening only like days,
That is, like holes, in a stuff where there is open work,
In a stuff, in an open-work texture.
It is night that is my great black wall,
Where days open only like windows
With a restless and flickering
And perhaps a false light,
Where days open only like days,
Where days open only like attic windows;
For it must not be said that the chain of times
Is comparable to an endless chain
In which link follows link, in which ring follows ring,
And days and nights are equal and follow each other in the same chain,
One white ring, one black ring, night hooking on today, day hooking on to night,
For they are not equal, they do not share the same dignity in that chain.
It is night that is continuous. It is night that forms the texture
Of time, the store of being,
And day looks out on that only through wretched windows and posterns.
It is day that disrupts, and day looks out on that
Only through sorry
Borrowed lights.[5] It is day that rends, and days are like isles in the sea,

---

5. One of Péguy's numerous plays on words. The French *jour de souffrance* may mean *borrowed light* as well as *day of suffering.*

Like interrupted isles that interrupt the sea,
But the sea continues and it is the isles that are wrong.
In the same way, the days are wrong, and interrupted
they interrupt night.
But no matter what they do, they themselves
Are immersed in the night. Just as the sea is the water
supply, so is night the reserve of being.
It is time which I have reserved for myself. All those
feverish days try in vain:
As on the high seas, right in the middle of night, they
are immersed in the depth of night.
It is they that are dispersed, they that are broken up.
Days are scattered bodies, night is the open sea.
In which Saint Paul sailed,
And the border that comes down from night towards
day
Is always an ascending border,
An abrupt border, and the border that re-ascends from
day towards night
Is always a descending border, in the depth of night.
O night, my most beautiful invention, my creation
august among all,
My most beautiful creature, creature of the greatest
Hope,
Giving most substance to Hope,
You who are the instrument, who are the very sub-
stance and abode of Hope,
And also (and thus), are really the creature of greatest
Charity,
For it is you who rock all Creation to sleep,

A refreshing sleep,
Just as one puts a child in his little bed,
Just as his mother puts him to bed, just as his mother tucks him in
And kisses him (she is not afraid of waking him.
He sleeps so soundly),
Just as his mother tucks him in and laughs and kisses him on the brow,
Enjoying it,
And he too laughs, he laughs in response as he sleeps;
Thus, O night, black-eyed mother, universal mother,
Not only mother of children (that is so easy),
But mother of men themselves and of women, which is so difficult,
It is you, night, who put to bed and make all Creation lie down
In a bed of a few hours
(In the meantime), in a bed of a few hours,
An image, a feeble image, and a promise and a realization beforehand of the bed of all the hours,
An anticipated realization, a promise held in advance,
While waiting for the bed of all hours,
In which I, the Father, will put my creation.
O Night, you are the night. And all those days together
Are never the day, they are never anything but days,
Sown. Those days are never anything but lights,
Uncertain lights, and you, night, you are my great dark light.
I congratulate myself on having made night. Days are islets and isles

That pierce and rend the sea,
But they have to rest in the deep sea,
They are compelled to do so.
Thus, you, days, are compelled,
You have to rest in the deep night,
And you, night, are the deep sea
In which Saint Paul sailed, no longer that little lake of Tiberias.
All those days are never anything but limbs
Dismembered. It is the days that emerge, but they have to be fixed in deep water,
In deep night. Night, my most beautiful invention, it is you who calm, it is you who soothe, it is you who put to rest
The aching limbs
All disjointed by the day's work.
It is you who calm, it is you who soothe, it is you who put to rest
The aching hearts,
The bruised bodies, the limbs bruised by toil, the hearts bruised by toil
And by trouble and daily care.
O Night, O my daughter Night, the most religious of my daughters,
The most pious;
Of all my daughters, of all my creatures, you are the one who is most in my hands, the one who most completely yields;
You glorify me in Sleep even more than your Brother Day glorifies me in Work,

For in work, man glorifies me only by his work,
And in sleep, it is I who glorify myself by the yielding of man,
And it is safer, I know better how to manage that.
Night, you are for man a food more nourishing than bread and wine,
For if he who eats and drinks does not sleep, he will derive no benefit from his food,
It will turn to sourness and make him sick;
But if he sleeps, bread and wine will become his flesh and blood,
To work, to pray, to sleep.
Night, you are the only one who dress wounds,
Aching hearts, all disjointed, all dismembered.
O my black-eyed daughter, you alone among my daughters who are, who can call yourself my accomplice,
Who acts in complicity with me, for you and I, I through you,
Together we cause man to fall in the snare of my arms
And take him somewhat by surprise,
But one takes him as best one can. If someone knows that, it is I.
Night, you are a beautiful invention
Of my wisdom.
Night, O my daughter Night, O my silent daughter,
At Rebecca's well, at the Samaritan woman's well,
It is you who draw the deepest water
From the deepest well;
O night, you who put all creatures to sleep,

A refreshing sleep,
O night, you who wash all wounds
In the only fresh water, in the only deep water,
At Rebecca's well, drawn from the deepest well;
Friend of children, friend and sister of young Hope,
O night, you who dress all wounds,
You who, at the Samaritan woman's well, draw from the deepest well
The deepest prayer,
O night, O my daughter Night, you who know how to hold your peace, O my daughter of the beautiful mantle,
You who shed rest and oblivion, you who shed balm, and silence, and darkness,
O my starry Night, I created you first.
You who put to sleep, you who, already, in an eternal Darkness bury
All my creatures,
The most restless, the spirited horse, the hardworking ant,
And man, that monster of restlessness,
Night, you who succeed in putting to sleep man,
That well of restlessness,
More restless in himself than all creation put together,
Man, that well of restlessness,
Just as you put to sleep the water in the well.
O my night of the long robe,
You who gather children and young Hope
In the folds of your robe,
But men won't allow themselves to be treated thus,

O my beautiful night, I created you first,
And almost before that,
Silent one of the long veils,
You by whom there comes down on earth a foretaste,
You who spread with your hands, you who shed on earth
A first peace,
    Forerunner of eternal peace,
A first rest,
    Forerunner of eternal rest,
A first balm, so cool, a first beatitude,
    Forerunner of eternal beatitude,
You who soothe, you who smell sweet, you who comfort,
You who dress wounds and bruised limbs,
You who put hearts to sleep, you who put bodies to sleep,
Aching hearts, aching bodies,
Bodies all stiff,
Limbs overwhelmed with fatigue, backs broken with weariness,
With tiredness, with cares, with restlessness,
Mortal restlessness,
With troubles,
You who shed balm on throats rent by bitterness,
Such a cool balm,
O my daughter of the great heart, I created you first,
Almost before the first, my daughter of the limitless bosom,
And well I knew what I was doing,

Perchance I knew what I was about;
You who lay the child in his mother's arms,
The child suffused with light by a shadow of sleep,
All laughter within himself, secretly laughing because
  of his confidence in his mother
And in me,
Secretly laughing with a serious pucker of his lips,
You who lay the child that is replete and overflowing
  with innocence
And confidence,
In his mother's arms.
You who lay the child Jesus every evening
In the arms of the Very Holy and Immaculate one,
You who are the portress of Hope,
O my daughter, first among all, you who succeed even,
  in this,
You who sometimes succeed, in this,
You who lay man in the arms of my Providence,
My maternal Providence,
O my *dark and gleaming daughter*, I greet you,
You who restore, you who nourish, you who rest,
O silence of darkness,
Such a silence reigned before the creation of unrest,
Before the beginning of the reign of unrest,
Such a silence will reign, but it will be a silence of light,
When all that unrest is brought to an end,
When all that unrest is exhausted,
When they have drawn all the water from the well,
After the end, after the exhaustion of all that unrest
Of man.

Thus, daughter, you are ancient and you are late,
For in this reign of unrest, you call to mind, you commemorate, you almost establish anew,
You almost cause to begin again the former Quietude
When my spirit moved upon the face of the waters.
But also, my starry daughter, daughter of the dark mantle, you are very much ahead of time, you are very precocious,
For you announce, for you represent, you almost cause to begin, ahead of time, every evening,
My great Quietude of light,
Of eternal light.
Night, you are holy, Night, you are great, Night, you are beautiful,
Night of the great mantle.
Night, I love you and greet you, and I glorify you, and you are my big daughter and my creature.
O beautiful night, night of the great mantle, daughter of the starry mantle,
You remind me, even me, you remind me of that great silence there was
Before I had opened up the floodgates of ingratitude,
And you announce to me, even me, you announce the great silence there will be
When I will have closed them.
O sweet, O great, O holy, O beautiful night, perhaps the holiest of my daughters, night of the long robe, of the starry robe,
You remind me of that great silence there was in the world

Before the beginning of the reign of man.
You announce to me that great silence there will be
After the end of the reign of man, when I will have resumed my scepter.
And at times I think of it beforehand, for that man really makes a lot of noise.
But specially, Night, you remind me of that night,
And I shall remember it eternally:
The ninth hour had struck. It was in the land of my people Israel.
All was over. That enormous adventure.
From the sixth hour, there had been darkness over all the land until the ninth hour.
All was over. Let us not mention it anymore. It hurts me.
That unbelievable coming down of my son among men,
In the midst of men,
When you think what they made of it,
Those thirty years during which he was a carpenter among men,
Those three years during which he was a kind of preacher among men,
A priest,
Those three days during which he was a victim among men,
In the midst of men,
Those three nights during which he was a dead man among men,
In the midst of dead men,

Those centuries and centuries when he is a host
among men.
All was over, that unbelievable adventure
By which I, God, have tied my arms for my eternity,
That adventure by which my Son tied my arms,
For eternally tying the arms of my justice, for eternally
untying the arms of my mercy,
And against my justice inventing a new justice,
A justice of love, a justice of Hope. All was over.
That which was necessary. In the way that was
necessary. In the way my prophets had announced
it. The veil of the temple was rent in twain from top
to bottom;
The earth did quake; the rocks rent;
The graves were opened; and many of the bodies of the
saints which slept arose.
And about the ninth hour, my Son uttered
The cry that will never be still. All was over. The
soldiers returned to their barracks,
Laughing and joking because that duty was over,
One more guard duty they would not have to stand.
Only one centurion remained, with a few men,
A very small post to guard that unimportant gallows,
The gallows on which my Son was hanged.
A few women only had remained.
The Mother was there.
And perhaps a few disciples too, and even so, one is not
sure of that.
Now every man has the right to bury his son,
Every man on earth, if he has had that great misfortune

Not to have died before his son. And I alone, I, God,
Arms tied by that adventure,
I alone, at that moment, father after so many fathers,
I alone could not bury my son.
It was then, O night, that you came,
O my daughter, beloved among all, and I still see it, and I shall see that in my eternity.
It was then, O Night, that you came, and in a great shroud you buried
The centurion and his Romans,
The Virgin and the holy women,
And that mountain, and that valley on which evening was descending,
And my people Israel and the sinners, and together him who was dying, who had died for them,

And the men of Joseph of Arimathea who already were approaching,

Bearing the white shroud.

CLUNY MEDIA

Designed by Fiona Cecile Clarke, the Cluny Media *logo*
depicts a monk at work in the scriptorium,
with a cat sitting at his feet.

The monk represents our mission to emulate
the invaluable contributions of the monks
of Cluny in preserving the libraries of the West,
our strivings to know and love the truth.

The cat at the monk's feet is Pangur Bán, from the
eponymous Irish poem of the 9th century.
The anonymous poet compares his scholarly
pursuit of truth with the cat's happy hunting of mice.
The depiction of Pangur Bán is an homage to the work
of the monks of Irish monasteries and a sign
of the joy we at Cluny take in our trade.

"Messe ocus Pangur Bán,
cechtar nathar fria saindan:
bíth a menmasam fri seilgg,
mu memna céin im saincheirdd."

Printed in Great Britain
by Amazon

70650673R00108